MARKETPLACE GATEKEEPERS
DOMINION OVER DOMAINS

| Gatekeeper Series |

David Adeola

Copyright © 2019 by David Adeola

The moral right of the author has been asserted.
All rights reserved. No part of this publication may be reproduced, stored in a retrieval system, or transmitted, in any form or by any means, without the prior permission in writing of the publisher, nor be otherwise circulated in any form of binding or cover other than that in which it is published and without a similar condition including this condition being imposed on the subsequent publisher.

ISBN 978-1-9164811-2-1

A CIP catalogue record for this book is available from the British Library.

Iheringius
An imprint of
Joensuu Media Ltd
20-22 Wenlock Road
London
N1 7GU
England

iheringius.com

CONTENTS

Acknowledgements	5
Definitions	7
1. Dominion	11
2. God as Master and Money as the Servant	41
3. Learning to Give All	51
4. Render to Caesar the Things that Are Caesar's	73
5. Favour Has a Purpose	85
6. Thanksgiving Brings Multiplication	107
7. Moving from Self to Kingdom Mentality	121
8. Worship in Spirit and in Truth	133
9. Parable of the Ten Minas	147
10. Integrity and Kingdom Wealth	155
11. Rest	161
12. Cast Your Nets on the Other Side	171
Economic Evangelism	178

ACKNOWLEDGEMENTS

I give all the glory and all the honour and all the praise to the King of Kings, my Lord and Saviour who saved me and redeemed me and grants me the grace to be a son for His purpose and will on earth.

There are a few key people in my life who are always there and are encouragers in my life and always my champions in whatever the Lord has assigned for me to do.

I'll like to give my special thanks to Michael Fenton-Jones. Your wisdom and counsel are invaluable.

Thanks to my friend and prayer partner, who also happens to be my publisher, Marko Joensuu. I appreciate your prayers and admonition and encouragement always. This book is part of the fulfilment of your prophetic word to me. I love you and your family dearly.

Thanks to my very dear brother and friend Apostle Dr. George Annadorai. You have been an inspiration in my life and your relentless love for God and for those around you is unsurpassable. Thank you for all the help you render for my teaching ministry. Thanks for your contribution towards this book. I love you dearly.

Thanks to Pauline Graham, Kunle Agunsoye, Prof. Tony Ng, for your prayers and consistent encouragement that fuels and drives me to never look back.

Special thanks to my dear wife Adekunbi Adeola who gave me the space and the encouragement to write this book and is always rooting for me to be all that the Lord has called me to be. You are my biggest champion. Thank you. I love you and I am trusting the Lord the best is very much ahead of us.

DEFINITIONS

Below are definitions of some of the central concepts in the book.

DOMAIN

Your domain is the sphere of influence that the Lord has given to you. It can be your workplace where you spend close to or more than a third of your life. Most of us give a minimum of eight hours out of our daily twenty-four hours to our work. That is your domain and you can bear quite a lot of influence there.

We are called to rule over our domains spiritually. You must exercise spiritual authority over your domain at all times in the Spirit. Many events happening in your domain are physical manifestations from whoever is exercising spiritual authority over that domain.

DOMINION

Dominion is the first gift that God gave to man in Genesis 1. It is the power to govern all that the Lord has bestowed upon us without being domineering. It is the power and anointing to govern and rule over your domain.

You are or will be in charge of workers in your organisation or even the CEO in your own company. You must lead, instruct and direct, but all this is to be done in a humane way regardless of who you have charge over, because all men and women have been created in God's image.

GATES

In the Old Testament times, gates were the physical place where decisions were made and agreements completed. Today, gates might not look like gates, but they are places of influence where we are meant to exercise spiritual authority. They include our parliaments, governmental institutions, corporate headquarters, stock exchanges, courts, and so on. Generally, they are places where significant decisions are made, and it is the task of gatekeepers to influence and make these decisions.

MARKETPLACE GATEKEEPERS

Marketplace gatekeepers are those who are in charge —either spiritually or physically—of a business,

DEFINITIONS

office, bank, investment, factory and so on—generally people in charge of commercial activities.

The only reason why you are created in His image is so you can have dominion and exercise the possibilities of what God might require of you as you grow in faith.

CHAPTER 1
DOMINION

Why should it surprise us that the Lord would have us to take dominion in the marketplace? After all, taking dominion was the first commandment that God ever gave to man. God has dominion over everything, and He has given us the ability to have dominion.

Genesis 1:26-31 says:

> Then God said, "Let us make man in our image, after our likeness. And let them have dominion over the fish of the sea and over the birds of the heavens and over the livestock and over all the earth and over every creeping thing that creeps on the earth." So God created man in his own image, in the image of God he created him; male and female he created them. And God blessed them. And God said to them, "Be fruitful and multiply and fill the earth and subdue it, and have dominion over the fish of the sea and over the birds of the heavens and over every living thing that moves on the earth." And God said, "Behold, I have given you

> every plant yielding seed that is on the face of all the earth, and every tree with seed in its fruit. You shall have them for food. And to every beast of the earth and to every bird of the heavens and to everything that creeps on the earth, everything that has the breath of life, I have given every green plant for food." And it was so. And God saw everything that he had made, and behold, it was very good. And there was evening and there was morning, the sixth day.

Dominion was the first gift that God gave to man, and it seems as if God couldn't wait to grant it. Now, mankind lives in a fallen state hence our wielding of power can often be oppressive, but the history of man illustrates that whether a man follows Jesus or not, he still carries the authority for dominion.

But biblical dominion is really about the returning of our ability for dominion to be under submission to God.

To have dominion in a godly way is to rule without domineering and by always keeping in mind that those who we have been entrusted to lead are also made in the image of God. And if you have been called to be a marketplace gatekeeper, the chances are that you have been called to wield at least some power over some other men and women.

That is why we must unpack these verses in Genesis 1 to understand what the Lord is saying to us as believers and especially to those of us called to operate in the marketplace. So, before we move on, we must slow down.

Here is the Creator, the Almighty God, who has just created every living being and brought these created beings to man.

Genesis 2:19 says,

> Now out of the ground the Lord God had formed every beast of the field and every bird of the heavens and brought them to the man to see what he would call them. And whatever the man called every living creature that was its name.

That verse packs a punch and indicates the power God gave man over the animals by asking him to name them. Whereas God named heaven and earth, day and night, earth and seas, He let man name the animals.

God didn't need man to be part of this process of naming, but He chose it to be that way. And naming has power. Even today, scientists seek to control the created world through defining its elements. And Jesus cast out demonic spirits by naming them.

IN HIS IMAGE AND LIKENESS

First the Lord created man and woman in His image. This doesn't make us equal to God, but gives us a certain level of creativity, more than enough to change their world and have dominion. You have been created in His image, so that you can have dominion and exercise your creativity. And no matter how broken the image of God in us might be, every man and woman retain some level of creativity at least in some spheres of life—even if they haven't been redeemed by Christ. That is why even atheists can achieve significant things.

Then God blessed Adam and Eve and called them to be fruitful and multiply, and to have dominion over every living being.

Sometimes it is useful to look at the synonyms for a word, and the synonyms for *fruitful* include fruit-bearing, fertile, fecund, high-yielding, lush, abundant, prolific, bounteous and generative. And from the perspective of marketplace gatekeeping, many of these synonyms are fully applicable to business and finance.

Multiplication is different from *addition*. It is a Kingdom principle, and it shows the amazing and supernatural ability of God. 2 x 2 doesn't operate according to the same principle than 2 + 2, although their sum is the same! Often, when you operate according to the principles of multiplication, the benefits become apparent only later, because 1 x 1 is less than 1 + 1, but 2 x 3 is already more than 2 + 3.

We are capable of growth by addition, but supernatural multiplication is only possible with God.

To *subdue* means to overcome, quieten or bring under control.

DOMINION

Our *dominion* started with Adam naming every living creature that the Lord had created. This leaves me with awe, as I try to imagine a puny little man, totally clueless except that the Lord is with him and has given him control over this world.

There is another level to dominion, which is only available to the followers of Christ. It is letting the *dunamis* power of the Holy Spirit operate through us.

DOMINION VS. DOMINATION

But what does it mean to exercise the dominion mandate of Genesis 1 today in society where men don't only exercise power over nature but also over other men?

It is useful to separate the biblical concept of *dominion* from the worldly concept of *domination*. In church and society, we can often find ourselves in a place where we are actually dominating our fellow brethren without even realising it. God gave man authority over every living thing, but He didn't give man authority over another man. The initial dominion we see Adam having was over the animals and not over another man. Every man and woman have been created in the image of God and are equal before God. If both man and woman have been created in the image of God, then we have not been called to dominate but to love one another. We must use the power we have been given over other people responsibly.

Genesis 2:21–24 says,

> So the Lord God caused a deep sleep to fall upon the man, and while he slept took one of his ribs and closed up its place with flesh. And the rib that the Lord God had taken from the man he made into a woman and brought her to the man. Then the man said, "This at last is bone of my bones and flesh of my flesh; she shall be called Woman, because she was taken out of Man." Therefore a man shall leave his father and his mother and hold fast to his wife, and they shall become one flesh.

These verses and the creation process of the Help—woman—for Adam tell us something very important about the relationship between the sexes. If woman has been created from the rib of man, and she is "flesh of my flesh", then God didn't call man to dominate woman. Many men use Genesis 2 as an excuse to dominate women, but that clearly isn't the intended takeaway message. According to Genesis 2, the creation of Eve took place after Adam had exercised his dominion to name the livestock that God had created. But does he have dominion over his helpmate? No. They became one flesh! You love and cherish.

So, the point Genesis 2 makes about the relationship between man and woman is not that man was created first to dominate woman, but the opposite: woman is not a separate "species" from man, but created "of him"—and this is the only time woman has been born out of man and not the other way around!

Because every man and woman have been created in God's image, the dominion we have over things is not extended over the other images of God. So, we need to always have one thing as a frontlet before our eyes, and that is to love one another.

Jesus says in John 13:34-35:

> A new commandment I give to you, that you love one another: just as I have loved you, you also are to love one another. By this all people will know that you are my disciples, if you have love for one another.

Loving someone never leads to dominating them. Instead, it leads to service. Paul writes in Romans 12:10: "Love one another with brotherly affection. Outdo one another in showing honor." So, rather than domineering we must compete in showing honour to each other. So, we must define the word "dominion" biblically as a positive word and see it in the light of the overall New Testament teaching, as part of our commission to exercise spiritual authority in the nations. But this authority is always for the betterment of the nations and not for their oppression.

Dominion means having the authority and the anointing to pray and declare God's will over a situation, as we are led by the Holy Spirit as intercessors and spiritual gatekeepers over our cities.

We must have dominion over the false ideologies that are being perpetrated by some of our politicians, and we must take that dominion in the Spirit, and that is by standing in the gap for our nation through persistent intercession, until we see a change for better.

Daniel exercised spiritual dominion over the situation in Babylon. But this spiritual dominion didn't just arrive by itself. Instead, he received it through his obedience to God's will. Daniel 1:8 says,

> But Daniel resolved that he would not defile himself with the king's food, or with the wine that he drank. Therefore he asked the chief of the eunuchs to allow him not to defile himself.

Daniel did not succumb to the pagan ruling authority when it pressurised him to stop worshipping the God of Israel. He exercised this different spirit in all his dealings consistently, and the Lord positioned him eventually along with his friends Hananiah, Mishael and Azariah to a place of prominence.

Daniel 1:19–20 says,

DOMINION

And the king spoke with them, and among all of them none was found like Daniel, Hananiah, Mishael, and Azariah. Therefore they stood before the king. And in every matter of wisdom and understanding about which the king inquired of them, he found them ten times better than all the magicians and enchanters that were in all his kingdom.

Dominion is preceded by taking a righteous position and not minding the consequences. It is about knowing who you are, whose you are and fully trusting in whose you are.

JOSEPH'S RISE TO POWER

Joseph became the prime minister of Egypt and exercised dominion over all the domains in Egypt. He was the most unlikely person to rule, given his former lowly status as a shepherd of flock with his brothers. We must never despise the days of small beginnings! It doesn't matter where you are presently; you can still be ruling in the next season of your life.

Joseph was loved more than all the other sons by his father Jacob, who made him a coat of many colours (Genesis 37:3). So, there was favour on his life already from a very young age. And Joseph saw a dream (Genesis 37:1-11), like many of us have dreams for our lives, and having a dream about our future is not anything bad. Almost everything begins with a dream!

But Joseph shared his dream with the wrong crowd—the *wrong* investors—who in this case were his brothers. He wrongly assumed that they would be celebrating him, but instead, sharing his dream led to rejection. Far too often we are discouraged from following God-given dreams by the people we consider closest to us!

It seems that to Joseph's brothers his dreams were about the elder brothers serving Joseph, when, in fact, they were about Joseph exercising dominion over Egypt. But perhaps even Joseph got the purpose of the dreams wrong initially. But that was certainly not the right audience to help Joseph make his dream a reality. The dream was right, but Joseph shared it with the wrong investors!

And then he had another dream, and he went to the same audience! Perhaps he should have learned from the first attempt. But on the other hand, apart from his brothers, he could only share the dream with the sheep!

There is an important lesson here for all marketplace gatekeepers. We must learn to be discerning on who to share our God-inspired ideas with. It's something that we must carefully evaluate and pray about consistently. Don't share your big dreams until you sense peace over sharing your dream with those who are your destiny helpers that have been called to help you to actualise your dreams. Just remember, perhaps you have been also called to help actualise the dreams of your destiny helpers, so that you will become their destiny helper.

But be careful who you share your dreams with!

Genesis 39 tells how, after Joseph had been sold off by his brothers as a slave to the Ishmaelites, he was taken to Egypt and sold to Potiphar, an officer of Pharaoh and the captain of the guard.

Joseph was soon promoted, and Potiphar made him the overseer over all things, including all the wealth of his house. As an overseer he would have watched over the many slaves and servants of the household.

One could have thought his best days were here, but Joseph soon got into trouble not of his own making. Potiphar's wife tried to seduce him, and he ran away. Unfortunately, Joseph left his robe behind while trying to escape. She used this piece of garment to frame him, and he was put in prison. Joseph must have been an excellent overseer, as his master had mercy on him—he might as easily have had Joseph killed rather than be put into prison.

But nothing could stop the operation of favour in Joseph's life. Genesis 39:23 says that "the Lord was with him; and whatever he did, the Lord made it prosper." It should be our conviction that whenever the enemy rears his ugly head that the Lord is also with us. So, Joseph became the leader of the prisoners and was put in charge of them. The keeper of the prison trusted Joseph so much that he let Joseph run everything without inspecting anything that fell under his remit.

The enemy often comes when we are about to break through into the domain where God wants us to bear fruit and be in charge. We must never give in but hold on to our faith, knowing the Lord will always deliver us from the hands of the enemy. The Lord is with us always, and He has promised to never leave or forsake us. If you are having challenges at work, and it seems there is no way forward with your circumstances seemingly like a prison, you must hold on to the Word of God, and trust that there is a purpose for you where the Lord has placed you, and that what you are facing must be only temporary.

SEASONS AND TIMINGS

Ecclesiastes 3:1-8 says,

> For everything there is a season, and a time for every matter under heaven: a time to be born, and a time to die; a time to plant, and a time to pluck up what is planted; a time to kill, and a time to heal; a time to break down, and a time to build up.

Seasons are vital for us as the marketplace gatekeepers. There are seasons and timings that we must recognise. This is helpful, so we do not despair even when things don't seem to turn in our favour immediately. Difficult seasons are usually a time of growing in grace and favour, even when it doesn't feel that way.

Psalm 37:34 says,

> Wait on the Lord, and keep His way, and He shall exalt you to inherit the land; when the wicked are cut off, you shall see it.

If we wait on the Lord, He will exalt us. Psalm 143:8 says,

> Cause me to hear Your lovingkindness in the morning, for in You do I trust; cause me to know the way in which I should walk, for I lift up my soul to You.

Often the night seems long, but morning will come; continue to encourage yourself in the Lord in the process of waiting!

Joseph wasn't promoted just because God had favour on him, but also because he made himself ready by putting into full use the gifts God had given to him despite the circumstances.

Proverbs 22:29 (MSG) says,

> Observe people who are good at their work—skilled workers are always in demand and admired; they don't take a backseat to anyone.

The NKJV translation puts it this way:

> Do you see a man who excels in his work? He will stand before kings; he will not stand before unknown men.

Joseph's gifts and skills made way for him in prison, and he was not only chosen to lead in prison, but the gifts of God in him were put to good use, which eventually got him out. It was his gift of dream interpretation that took him before the Pharaoh and his skill of administration that gave him the position as the prime minister over Egypt.

Very often what we need when we are going through challenges is to harness the gifts of God that are in us and use them to the best of our ability. Rather than spending time in despair, put your skills into use, even when you are not in that desirable position, and allow the Lord to use your gifts to bring you out into a wealthy place.

Psalms 66:10-12 says,

> For you, O God, have tested us; you have tried us as silver is tried. You brought us into the net; you laid a crushing burden on our backs; you let men ride over our heads; we went through fire and through water; yet you have brought us out to a place of abundance.

When you are being tested, you can't rely on man to help solve your problem. And attempting to circumvent the test won't work either. But the writer of the psalm testifies that all suffering will eventually come to an end, and that after testing will come reward and promotion—if you learn to walk according to God's will!

Joseph had been in prison with the chief cupbearer to Pharaoh who had seen a dream which Joseph interpreted. Joseph tells him that he will be released from prison, and it happens exactly according to Joseph's interpretation. Joseph begs the chief cupbearer to remember him once he gets out of prison.

Yet the chief butler did not remember Joseph, but forgot him. (Genesis 40:23)

Joseph stays in prison for further two years. When we help others to achieve their dream, it can often seem that there is no payback for us, as those we have helped are not motivated by love but by self-interest, and they soon forget us.

But that doesn't mean that God has forgotten us. The appointed time comes with Pharaoh having seen a disturbing dream, which his magicians are unable to interpret.

At this appointed time the chief cupbearer remembers Joseph—perhaps as it now serves his self-interest! But God is well able to use anyone's self-interest. Suddenly Joseph's gift becomes relevant again, and he is invited to Pharaoh's court to interpret the dream.

MARKETPLACE GATEKEEPERS

Often, we have a sense that someone is meant to help us—but it is not yet God's appointed time! From human point of view, we are not in their list of priorities, so they forget us, until our gift becomes useful to them again. They have no ill feelings, but they are busy chasing their own destiny.

JOSEPH RULES EGYPT

Joseph's gift brought him before Pharaoh, and he interpreted the dream to Pharaoh with clarity. He told Pharaoh that there would be seven years of plenty followed by seven years of famine and explained what needed to be done to avert a disaster of an impending famine.

God had ordained what was about to happen, and no one could change it, but there was one wise person to whom God had given the wisdom, so the land would not perish through the famine. Joseph advised Pharaoh to gather and store during the coming seven years of plenty, so that there would be enough to eat during the subsequent seven years of lack.

And what came after is what every marketplace gatekeeper can only dream about!

> This proposal pleased Pharaoh and all his servants. And Pharaoh said to his servants, "Can we find a man like this, in whom is the Spirit of God?" Then Pharaoh said to Joseph, "Since God has shown you all this, there is none so discerning and

> wise as you are. You shall be over my house, and all my people shall order themselves as you command. Only as regards the throne will I be greater than you." And Pharaoh said to Joseph, "See, I have set you over all the land of Egypt. Then Pharaoh took his signet ring from his hand and put it on Joseph's hand, and clothed him in garments of fine linen and put a gold chain about his neck. And he made him ride in his second chariot. And they called out before him, "Bow the knee!" Thus he set him over all the land of Egypt. Moreover, Pharaoh said to Joseph, "I am Pharaoh, and without your consent no one shall lift up hand or foot in all the land of Egypt." (Genesis 41:37-44)

According to verses 41-44, all the authority in the land of Egypt had been handed over to Joseph. Joseph became the de facto no 1 man in the whole of Egypt. Above him was only Pharaoh, but he had delegated the running of the kingdom to Joseph. This former shepherd and slave was only thirty years old, but he had been given power over all things in the nation!

Joseph married and had a son named Manasseh, which means "God has made me forget all my hardship." And his second son was called Ephraim, which means "God has made me fruitful in the land of my affliction."

The spiritual principles outlined in Joseph's story are applicable to us in our workplaces and domains. Often, we will have to persevere and wait on the Lord for the right timing and right place for His perfect plan for our lives to be manifested. He does have a plan, but many of us don't like the waiting period and the challenges that encounter us!

As Joseph persevered in slavery and imprisonment, he was actually honing his God-given gifts. He became proficient in them to the point that it didn't only seem credible enough for Pharaoh to ask him for dream interpretation, but it also led to life transformation.

Our domain is that place where the Lord has positioned us. Domain is a territory owned or controlled by a particular ruler. This is shown in Jude 1:6, which says about the fallen angels: "And the angels who did not keep their proper domain, but left their own abode". Likewise, God has given us our proper domain, and we are meant to exercise spiritual authority over it: to keep it. We are to rule over a spiritual region, a territory.

Jesus said,

> With man it is impossible, but not with God. For all things are possible with God. (Mark 10:27)

You have spiritual dominion when you begin to understand and know you are made in the image of God and that with God nothing shall be impossible. When you grasp that you will spend less time thinking about the challenges and the impossibility of the task and focus on discovering God's plans and intentions.

DOMINION

Joseph applied God-given wisdom, and when the famine started, the whole earth came to Egypt to buy grains.

> Moreover, all the earth came to Egypt to Joseph to buy grain, because the famine was severe over all the earth. (Genesis 41:57)

The nation of Israel was preserved through this formidable act of Joseph. Israel settled in the land of Egypt and prospered and multiplied greatly.

Joseph not only preserved the known world from being devastated by hunger and famine through his business acumen, but he made so many profitable deals for Pharaoh that the he became even wealthier through the famine.

Genesis 47:23 gives us an important principle.

> Then Joseph said to the people, "Indeed I have bought you and your land this day for Pharaoh. Look, here is seed for you, and you shall sow the land."

The seed that was given to the people was meant to take them beyond the famine. There was the supply during the famine, so the people did not die, but there was the seed to live for afterwards.

This is an important message for us as marketplace gatekeepers. We must always have the seed and never consume everything we have but be able to secure something for the future that is beyond us and after us.

Joseph gave the people seed for harvest but made an agreement with them to give a fifth of whatever their harvest would bring to Pharaoh. This 20% tax became the law in Egypt. Joseph secured what would be a lifelong income for the household of Pharaoh.

Joseph wasn't simply concerned of the present time, but he seemed intent on leaving a legacy for future generations. Because he served Pharaoh, he left a great inheritance to the children of Pharaoh. Likewise, we must have the same mind-set of storing for the next generation at the times when things are going well. Whatever the Lord has given into our hands must not be all spent by us!

Proverbs 13:22 says,

> A good man leaves an inheritance to his children's children, but the sinner's wealth is laid up for the righteous.

Joseph was only able to achieve this because he exercised his power of dominion that gave him the authority to store in times of plenty in readiness for the time of famine. This saved the known world by preserving a generation and also the nation of Israel, so they could fulfil God's ultimate plan of salvation for all mankind. Joseph secured the future of Israel even when he knew that he wasn't going to be around to enjoy it. He didn't exercise dominion for himself only but also for the future of Israel.

But it is important to note Joseph's style of leadership that also led to complications for the future Israel. Joseph seems to have been so concerned about fulfilling the vision and the dream that there were moments when his style of being an overseer was clearly overbearing. The people cried out at some point because of the heavy burden that was placed upon them, perhaps paving the way to the subsequent slavery of the Israelites in Egypt.

This is something we must learn from as gatekeepers when God gives us a dream or a vision.

In many ways, Joseph was phenomenally successful in fulfilling the vision. Genesis 41:49 says,

> And Joseph stored up grain in great abundance, like the sand of the sea, until he ceased to measure it, for it could not be measured.

But when he traded the grain during famine, he was perhaps too excessive by forcing Egyptians to trade their land ownership for survival. He seemed rather ruthless in his dealings with the people. As Christians, we must never do likewise: we must never bring a burden or be domineering over the people we oversee.

However, while I do not entirely agree with all of Joseph's actions as leader, the time Joseph lived was an unprecedented time, and his goal was to preserve the nation—which happened but with some unforeseen consequences. He was a shrewd businessman, but although he brought the people to a position of servitude, he still gave them the seed to grow harvests beyond and after the famine.

However, we have learnt something very important from the life of Joseph: it wasn't just his gift but also his resilience and grit that put him through to Pharaoh. Joseph could have just whined about his condition, which he had not deserved, but he never gave up. And most of us will encounter dire circumstances at some point in our lives—perhaps not as extreme as Joseph did—but we must never give up!

Joseph never gave up regardless of the various challenges and even the attempt to frame him for rape. Instead, he stood with integrity even when he was punished for sin he didn't even commit.

But who can know the many lives that he must have touched during his journey to the palace to be a ruler in Egypt? As Joseph was a Jew, he was far from being the top candidate for the job, but God prepared him to be the solution to problems of the then known world! To do that, he must have solved a large number of smaller problems on the way.

DOMINION

Are you a Joseph in the marketplace? Are you in the marketplace just for yourself, or are you there to be the change for our crooked world by using the gifts and skills that the Lord has given you? Are you looking to better our world that is crying out for help, or are you just looking to make money?

God isn't working to accomplish short-term but long-term goals that extend our lifetime. If you are called to be a marketplace gatekeeper, the chances are that what you have been called to do is meant to become a legacy that will last long after you are gone for the sake of the Gospel and the Kingdom.

What challenges are you going through? Take a cue from the life of Joseph and begin to see the light.

DOMINION IS ABOUT SECURING YOUR INHERITANCE

When you begin to take dominion, you begin to secure your inheritance and the inheritance of the generations after you. And there is a domain for everyone to take authority over either in the marketplace or in the place of prayer and intercession for our cities.

But we need a lot of wisdom, as God's plan for each generation can be fulfilled in different ways. The Lord told Jacob's father Isaac to remain in the land and not leave despite the famine in the land. In fact, He explicitly commanded Isaac not to go to Egypt. The Lord provided for him and then Isaac became very wealthy in the land. But then he led Jacob's son Joseph to Egypt to make way for Jacob and his sons to leave the land! It seems that what is disobedient in one season can be obedient in another!

However, what I'm getting on to is more than just Isaac being wealthy—his life was all about the inheritance. The inheritance that was Isaac's was through his father also became ours because of the covenant God made with Abraham. But that was something he had to exercise dominion over. It didn't come to him automatically.

There was battle over that inheritance. Abraham had dug wells in Beersheba in Genesis 21 as witness for his agreement with King Abimelech. These wells had been blocked by the Philistines after Abraham's death. But in Genesis 26 we find Isaac reopening the wells again but with local herdsmen taking over them, as they wanted to benefit from Isaac's labour.

One could have thought that Abraham digging the wells would have been the end of it, but the drama of digging the wells was being replayed in Isaac's generation.

Isaac and his servants kept on digging the wells and there was contention each time, but they kept on re-digging the wells of his father Abraham until there was no contention. It seems that the enemy doesn't respect our rights for inheritance. But it would have been easier to re-dig the wells as Isaac would have already known where the water was, so he benefited greatly from Abraham's earlier search for water.

Now this is an inheritance which goes beyond just riches and wealth. It was an inheritance that still belongs to us today because the promise of the Lord was to Abraham's generation and to all who have over the centuries received God's righteousness by faith and not by the works of the law. This is an inheritance that has blessed the whole world, and it continues to bless us today!

It wasn't an easy contention, but perhaps Joseph's resilience had also been inherited from Isaac. Despite the contentions Isaac and his servants never stopped digging until they finally made it to Beersheba where Abraham had made a covenant with King Abimelech, planted a tamarisk tree and dug a well.

It is here that God appears to Isaac and reminds him of the covenant that He has made with Abraham—and because of Abraham with Isaac and his offspring. Then King Abimelech who made an oath and a covenant with Abraham comes to make a covenant with Isaac also, as he has seen that God is also with Isaac.

In the verse 29 King Abimelech says to Isaac, "You are now the blessed of the Lord."

This is the place of the oath and covenant. Not only does God remind Isaac of his covenant, but also the most influential men of the region—people who have earlier pushed him away—acknowledge God's favour over his life and want to partake in it! Abimelech wants to make a covenant with Isaac because he can see that God has made a covenant with Isaac.

This is the place where we arrive after many troubles if we haven't allowed the trouble to stop us from pursuing our goal and ultimately our inheritance, because we believe in the promises of God—no matter what comes our way. This is about us knowing what belongs to us and going after it.

This perseverance is the mind-set of a true marketplace gatekeeper.

Isaac was not going after something that was not his. He was operating under the oath and covenant of God that was over his father Abraham but had now been passed on to him. In Genesis 26:3-5 God tells Isaac:

> Sojourn in this land, and I will be with you and will bless you, for to you and to your offspring I will give all these lands, and I will establish the oath that I swore to Abraham your father. I will multiply your offspring as the stars of heaven and will give to your offspring all these lands. And in your offspring all the nations of the earth shall be blessed, because Abraham obeyed my voice and kept my charge, my commandments, my statutes, and my laws.

DOMINION

The apostle Paul says in Galatians 3:29, "If you are Christ's, then you are Abraham's offspring, heirs according to promise." We are also Abraham's offspring and under the same covenant and oath for the blessings of God through Abraham.

Isaac simply needed to go after what belonged to him, but the enemy was always on the prowl to attack and dispossess Isaac of his inheritance, which is not different with us now.

God's oath and covenant are everlasting but often we also must pursue and fight for them. Isaac pursued them, until he got to a place where there was no longer any contention for what was now clearly his inheritance. Genesis 26:22 says,

> And he moved from there and dug another well, and they did not quarrel over it. So he called its name Rehoboth, saying, "For now the Lord has made room for us, and we shall be fruitful in the land."

This same covenant operated also through Joseph because of God's covenant for the children of Israel through Abraham, Isaac and Jacob. Joseph went through extreme difficulties, but there was a purpose in it, and not once did he lose hope, and eventually he came to understand that he was a forerunner for the people of Israel in the land of Egypt.

In Genesis 45:4–8 Joseph, now the ruler of Egypt, reveals himself to his brothers:

> So Joseph said to his brothers, "Come near to me, please." And they came near. And he said, "I am your brother, Joseph, whom you sold into Egypt. And now do not be distressed or angry with yourselves because you sold me here, for God sent me before you to preserve life. For the famine has been in the land these two years, and there are yet five years in which there will be neither plowing nor harvest. And God sent me before you to preserve for you a remnant on earth, and to keep alive for you many survivors. So it was not you who sent me here, but God. He has made me a father to Pharaoh, and lord of all his house and ruler over all the land of Egypt."

Joseph had been sent ahead by God to preserve a generation because of the oath and the covenant that the Lord had made with Abraham. Whatever trouble and trials he had gone through now seemed insignificant to him because of the ultimate purpose of God expressed in His promise to Abraham. And this promise is unchangeable and is everlasting!

LESSONS

Never give up! Your position in Christ works beyond you, because your life is not just about you but also about the inheritance for those who come after you.

DOMINION

Your life has been purposed to bless many generations after you—long after you are gone.

Recommended reading: *Genesis 37-48*.

―⊷⊶―

The principle of radical generosity doesn't apply only to the rich but also to the poor. No matter who you are, giving is a key ingredient of living in God's favour.

―⊷⊶―

CHAPTER 2
GOD AS MASTER AND MONEY AS THE SERVANT

> No servant can serve two masters, for either he will hate the one and love the other, or he will be devoted to the one and despise the other. You cannot serve God and money. (Luke 16:13)

> How could you worship two gods at the same time? You will have to hate one and love the other, or be devoted to one and despise the other. You can't worship the true God while enslaved to the god of money! (Matthew 6:24 TPT)

There are many Christians in the marketplace who are totally unaware of their position in the realm of the Spirit and why they are where they are. We are not called to serve or be enslaved by *mammon* as many do today. Instead, the Lord wants mammon (an Aramaic word for money) to serve the Kingdom of God.

There can be only one master, and if Jesus is our Master, then money must be our servant! But the work of the Kingdom is being stifled due to lack of finances which are still in the hands of either unbelievers or Christians who are unaware of what the purpose behind their wealth is. But the bottom line is that finances that are very much needed for the work of the Kingdom appear to be in the wrong hands at the gates—hands that are not serving God but mammon.

The mandate in Matthew 28:18-20 to go and make disciples is much more than just evangelism:

> And Jesus came and said to them, "All authority in heaven and on earth has been given to me. Go therefore and make disciples of all nations, baptizing them in the name of the Father and of the Son and of the Holy Spirit, teaching them to observe all that I have commanded you. And behold, I am with you always, to the end of the age."

The Great Commission asks us to go to nations and make disciples. But what kind of disciples has Jesus asked us to make? Disciples that will obey all He has instructed us to do. This means going beyond the four walls of the church building.

One of the ways of achieving this is to raise marketplace gatekeepers who will become the hands and feet of Jesus to enable the evangelist to go, to allow the teacher to teach and the prophet to go to the nations of the world without any financial hindrances. The marketplace gatekeepers are enablers who are God's stewards of financial resources for the expansion of God's Kingdom on earth.

And what happens when people working in the government, Parliament, education or business become disciples? They begin to operate in those spheres following the principles and the values of God's Kingdom.

The word "teach" in this verse is about mentoring the next generation by not only making the Word of God known but ensuring that it is kept.

In Matthew 24:14 Jesus says,

> And this gospel of the kingdom will be proclaimed throughout the whole world as a testimony to all nations, and then the end will come.

The marketplace gatekeepers are an integral part of God's end time plan to facilitate all that the Church needs to do to prepare for Jesus's second coming. What a privilege to be part of this as a gatekeeper!

Solomon writes in Ecclesiastes 10:19,

> Bread is made for laughter, and wine gladdens life, and money answers everything.

Looking at life, King Solomon acknowledges the vital role money plays. This is a simple observation that doesn't justify greed. But in our society, it is impossible to do anything without money. We need money to preach the gospel, visit and look after the orphans, or, for example, to buy TV airtime for Christian programmes. Many great plans of being the salt and light for the world are stifled by the lack of finances.

Obviously, money is not an end in itself, and we trust God and look up to Him alone. But so often, the answer to our prayers seems to come through the generosity of God's servants. And God has called some to be in the position as enablers to facilitate the provision for all of God's kingdom endeavours. These gatekeepers will see God as Master and money as the servant.

But being a marketplace gatekeeper isn't just about raising money. God wants to raise up gatekeepers in the marketplace to be people of influence. This is only possible if we begin to recognise that our Kingdom mandate truly extends beyond our church buildings. If you are already positioned in the marketplace, you need to understand why you are there. You aren't just making a career for yourself in business, banking, the legal system and so on as a Christian, and then put money in the offering bucket on Sunday as an overflow of your blessing. You aren't just called to take from the plenty of the marketplace and bring it to bless the Church, but you are also called to influence the marketplace and how it functions.

1 Chronicles 9:26-27 says about Solomon's Temple,

> For the four chief gatekeepers, who were Levites, were entrusted to be over the chambers and the treasures of the house of God. And they lodged around the house of God, for on them lay the duty of watching, and they had charge of opening it every morning.

The verse 33 adds,

> Now these, the singers, the heads of fathers' houses of the Levites, were in the chambers of the temple free from other service, for they were on duty day and night.

These gatekeepers were priests. The Levites, who were the gatekeepers of the Temple, had charge over the treasuries of the house of God. We can see how in the Temple mammon was subject to God. It served God's purposes.

These Levites had a very specific call, and God had separated them for that purpose. In a similar vein, God has called and anointed some to operate in the marketplace to be stewards of God's resources for the end-time harvest. Like in the Temple, God wants to subject mammon through His servants today, so that it will achieve His purposes.

We need to take possession of the gates, because we are yet to finish with our commission of taking the Gospel to all the nations. Like I said, a marketplace gatekeeper isn't just making money in the marketplace; he or she is also influencing how the market functions. He or she is there to open and shut the door.

Today, the gates to some of the nations are firmly shut, and it takes prayer and financing to reach out to these people. For example, in the Middle East the Gospel has been preached effectively in the last few years through the internet and satellite TV. We can see clearly how God is using media to bring many to the truth of the Lord Jesus, and the testimonies of salvation we have heard have been nothing short of amazing. But this work takes a lot of finance.

Marketplace gatekeepers are intercessors and watchmen, so if you are called to become one, you must learn to pray and be a worshipper. As you have seen, the gatekeepers who were treasurers in the House of God were Levites.

It is not enough to operate in the marketplace, it is only enough to operate in the marketplace *with* the Lord.

Taking possession of the gates is not dominion theology—a theocratic ideology that seeks to implement a nation governed by Christians ruling over the rest of society. Instead, it is about walking in the promises of God.

HOW DO WE DO ALL THIS?

We need to develop an awareness and discernment of where we are presently and understand how the enemy possesses our gates. We also need to walk in obedience. This is not sin-free perfection but like the obedience of Abraham, which means trusting in what God has promised to us and taking practical action because of His promises.

We need teachers and mentors who understand what the gates are in the marketplace and how to take possession of them.

We must begin to gather the Christians who have been called and commissioned by God to operate in the marketplace. Church has largely ignored this area, and, consequently, many Christians working in the marketplace don't see their work as a calling and as part of the expansion of the Kingdom. A religious mind-set separates the sacred from the secular, but in God's eyes all our life can and should be a service to Him.

One area of my calling is to travel to bring an awareness to the gatekeepers in the nations and impart what the Lord has taught me into them so they could take a stand for their nations. This costs money. We are not able to ride donkeys to the nations, and many are unable to fulfil this mandate to teach and disciple the nations.

Psalm 24:1 says,

> The earth is the Lord's and the fullness thereof, the world and those who dwell therein.

This is a fundamental truth, but today, we can see how Satan—the thief—has got in the possession of many of those "who dwell therein." And we don't see the marketplace in God's possession. But as we walk with God, we can begin to exercise spiritual authority wherever we go—including the marketplace!

But often we look for the wrong people for guidance. A preacher might be able to give you a good sermon, but it takes someone in the marketplace to show and mentor other people in the same field.

It takes intentional action to lay hold of the gates of our city and nation. One man is doing amazing things with the resources the Lord has placed in his hands to change our world as we know it for good. That man is Bill Gates, known as William Henry Gates III, who has the rather bold and audacious ambition to eradicate four known world diseases like malaria, which is preventable and treatable, by 2030, just as smallpox, polio and Guinea-worm disease are, and is making a major impact with landmark results showing the possibilities we have as gatekeepers.

Gates states in regard to his faith: "The moral systems of religion, I think, are super important.

We've raised our kids in a religious way; they've gone to the Catholic Church that Melinda goes to and I participate in. I've been very lucky, and therefore I owe it to try and reduce the inequity in the world. And that's kind of a religious belief. I mean, it's at least a moral belief."

The Bill Gates Foundation is a worldwide initiative already making its mark in affecting our world in a very remarkable way. And it is doing amazing things just because one man has decided to apply biblical principles even when he doesn't seem to be quite certain about the exact object of his faith. Imagine how much more we can do as gatekeepers when we put our full trust in the Lord and seek to apply all that He has written!

For because of this you also pay taxes, for the authorities are ministers of God, attending to this very thing. Pay to all what is owed to them: taxes to whom taxes are owed, revenue to whom revenue is owed, respect to whom respect is owed, honor to whom honor is owed. (Romans 13:6-7)

CHAPTER 3
LEARNING TO GIVE ALL

One day a wealthy Jewish nobleman of high standing posed this question to Jesus: "Wonderful Teacher, what must I do to be saved and receive eternal life?" Jesus answered, "Why would you call me wonderful when there is only one who is wonderful—and that is God alone? You already know what is right and what the commandments teach: 'Do not commit adultery, do not murder, do not steal, do not lie, and respectfully honor your father and your mother.'"

The wealthy leader replied, "These are the very things I've been doing for as long as I can remember." Ah," Jesus said. "But there's still one thing you're missing in your life."

"What is that?" asked the man. "You must go and sell everything you own and give all the proceeds to the poor so you will have eternal treasures. Then come and follow me."

When the rich leader heard these words, he was devastated, for he was extremely wealthy. Jesus saw his disappointment, and looking right at him he said, "It is next to impossible for those who have everything to enter into God's kingdom realm. Nothing could be harder! It could be compared to trying to stuff a rope through the eye of a needle." Those who heard this said, "Then who can be saved?" (Luke 18:18-25 TPT)

Giving away all your wealth is one of the greatest tests for anyone in the marketplace. But dare I say that you cannot be a tool in the hands of God if you are not one with a generous heart? And through the Bible we can see how the Lord truly blesses our generosity.

One might ask why this rich marketplace ruler asked a question like this from Jesus. Was he genuinely looking for an assurance that he could inherit an eternal life? Or did he think that he already had eternal life in his possession?

Was he a disciple? It seems that he at least wanted to be one. And he seemed to be the embodiment of the Jewish understanding of righteousness: a man who had been blessed by God because of his righteous deeds. But something was missing. He wanted more. He wanted to be a disciple of Jesus. But the price tag was too high.

But it is not all bad news for us! Being in the marketplace as a disciple of Jesus does have its advantages over those who don't know the Lord at all. Marketplaces have many gatekeepers, and most of them are not following Jesus. This rich gatekeeper had just asked a fatal question. *What does it mean to follow*

LEARNING TO GIVE ALL

Jesus? And Jesus's response was that if this rich man wanted to follow Him, he would first need to follow Him in his dealings at the marketplace. We don't know how this young ruler had earned his money. But Jesus clearly wanted to give it away.

The rich ruler very clearly believed in the Mosaic Law, and he thought that he had kept all the commandments. And he clearly believed in the teachings of Jesus at least to some level.

Jesus set the ultimate test of the heart to the rich marketplace ruler. First, He asked if the rich ruler had kept all the commandments. The rich ruler answered affirmatively.

The rich ruler must have felt very pleased with himself! Like the rich ruler, we can be so self-absorbed that we think we are doing God a favour by showing up in church on a Sunday and giving our tithes and offerings.

The rich ruler seemed very conversant with the Law.

But Jesus was not finished with him. He said, "One thing you still lack. Sell all that you have and distribute to the poor, and you will have treasure in heaven; and come, follow me."

If we are truly honest with ourselves, most of us would admit that Jesus was asking for far too much! As did the rich ruler; he became sad as he was "extremely" rich.

This was not just some CEO or General Manager who was paid a monthly salary but a mega-rich ruler in the marketplace. This was the Bill Gates or the Warren Buffet of that time! He was stupendously rich.

What Jesus was highlighting was that the rich young ruler had not in fact followed the law completely. Perhaps he had fulfilled the Law mechanically, but not in his heart, because his wealth and riches had become his god.

His love for money had over time replaced God in his heart. It had become his idol. He couldn't part with what he thought he had acquired to follow God fully.

If we read through the Ten Commandments in Exodus 20, we realise that this rich ruler was probably flouting at least four commandments. In his mind, he had kept the commandments that Jesus had listed. But there were other commandments regarding idolatry, worshipping other gods (money, etc.), and against covetousness, and the rich man was breaking them at least in his heart.

Most of us would have had difficulties in obeying this command of Jesus to give away all. And the Lord knows our hearts, and nothing is hidden from Him. But Jesus wasn't so much interested in taking away all that the rich man had; He was searching his heart and the grip his riches had on him. Likewise, He often reveals to us what really rules our hearts and what motivates us to do what we are doing.

LEARNING TO GIVE ALL

After the rich man had gone away in sorrow Jesus explained to His disciples that it was difficult for a rich man to enter the Kingdom of God.

I don't think this story can be used to teach that Jesus is against Christians being wealthy. But He is concerned of our salvation and wants to set us free. The rich ruler's response demonstrates that he was more concerned about his riches than truly obeying God's commandments. His riches were his god.

Jesus was really dealing with two separate issues simultaneously: our salvation and the principles of the Kingdom.

And it seems that the disciples got the wrong end of the stick. We must understand that, like most Jews, the disciples would have believed that the rich man's wealth was an external sign of his righteousness. So, they were amazed: if the rich man couldn't be saved, how could anyone?

> Jesus responded: "What is impossible with man is possible with God." (Luke 18:27)

Rich or poor—it is impossible for a man to save himself. And it was Jesus' mission to bring us salvation. He made the impossible possible. So, clearly Jesus wasn't expecting the rich man to save himself by giving away all his riches.

But the rich man's predicament still troubled Peter. Even if the rich man couldn't save himself by giving away his riches, the fact remains that Jesus did ask him to give them away and follow Jesus. It seems that Peter was trying to figure out his position in the Kingdom.

> And Peter said, "See, we have left our homes and followed you." And he said to them, "Truly, I say to you, there is no one who has left house or wife or brothers or parents or children, for the sake of the kingdom of God, who will not receive many times more in this time, and in the age to come eternal life." (Luke 18:28-30 ESV)

God is not a debtor to any man! He gives back more than we can ever ask of Him. The important lesson here is that our salvation is more important than our riches. Our wealth or riches should never take the place of God as our provider.

And yes, our riches can be a sign of God's favour. Someone else might try to do what you did with no success, but it is working for you, not because of your smartness but because of His grace and favour!

So, Jesus is not asking us not to do business, but that we should operate in the marketplace the more excellent way, in righteousness. He is in the business of bringing the Kingdom into the marketplace and not just trying to help us get rich!

LEARNING TO GIVE ALL

We need to learn to serve Him rather than money as our master even when in the marketplace. Too many Christians serve God in church and money in the marketplace. But God wants us to serve *Him* in the marketplace.

But as Jesus said, whatever we give to Him, He will give back to us—but in greater measure! This promise should give us the confidence to live with radical generosity.

Jesus says in Luke 6:30 (ESV):

> Give to everyone who begs from you, and from one who takes away your goods do not demand them back.

Jesus says in Luke 6:38,

> Give, and it will be given to you. Good measure, pressed down, shaken together, running over, will be put into your lap. For with the measure you use it will be measured back to you.

This principle of radical generosity doesn't apply only to the rich but also to the poor. No matter who you are, giving is a key ingredient of living in God's favour.

Again, Luke 21:1-4 makes the same point.

> Jesus looked up and saw the rich putting their gifts into the offering box, (and he saw a poor widow put in

two small copper coins. And he said, "Truly, I tell you, this poor widow has put in more than all of them. For they all contributed out of their abundance, but she out of her poverty put in all she had to live on."

It's not very often we see a pastor having a close look into how much we are putting in the offering box! I think most of us would be offended by this kind of scrutiny. But thank God Jesus did, so we are able to draw wisdom from the story.

Jesus didn't want so much to know about the amount but the heart of the giver. He was highlighting the sacrificial giving and the sincerity of the poor widow's heart. The widow gave all that she had despite being as poor as anyone can be. The rich gave numerically much more but in God's eyes much less, because they gave from their plenty. However, the others who gave numerically much more would probably have been more generous in the eyes of a pastor.

The rich gave little out of their abundance. The widow had an abundant mentality, and she gave abundantly from her little. She knew that the Lord who had provided for her was able to do so again. She was not fearful but had an absolute confidence in the Provider!

There is no need to live under condemnation when it comes to your giving. There is no compulsion but freedom in giving. But I do believe the Lord would want

LEARNING TO GIVE ALL

us to cultivate a heart of generosity and an abundant mentality to be able to give beyond and above what we are giving now. And this doesn't necessarily have to be in a church setting. Our generosity can be extended in many areas of society! Many of us already support charities and other initiatives that alleviate poverty and help orphans and widows.

All I can say is that don't ever stop being a giver with an abundant mentality. Know that the Lord can abound His grace to you in an unprecedented way!

Paul writes about the Macedonian Christians:

> For in a severe test of affliction, their abundance of joy and their extreme poverty have overflowed in a wealth of generosity on their part. For they gave according to their means, as I can testify, and beyond their means, of their own accord, begging us earnestly for the favor of taking part in the relief of the saints (2 Corinthians 8:2-4)

This kind of giving is only possible when it is motivated by love and encouraged by the confidence that God will be able to replenish our supply.

Our giving is an act of worship, as we see in the story of the woman with the alabaster box.

> A woman came up to him with an alabaster flask of very expensive ointment, and she poured it on his

head as he reclined at table. And when the disciples saw it, they were indignant, saying, "Why this waste? For this could have been sold for a large sum and given to the poor." But Jesus, aware of this, said to them, "Why do you trouble the woman? For she has done a beautiful thing to me. For you always have the poor with you, but you will not always have me. In pouring this ointment on my body, she has done it to prepare me for burial. Truly, I say to you, wherever this gospel is proclaimed in the whole world, what she has done will also be told in memory of her." (Matthew 26:7-13)

Here is a woman who was able to release all that she had and pour it on Jesus as an act of worship. But even the disciples were so indignant of what they described as "waste". One could have imagined that the disciples should have welcomed this act, as they had followed Jesus for the last three years. But what suddenly sprang up was their business mind-set that did all the calculations on how the proceeds would have been distributed to the poor. Don't forget that these men operated in the marketplace as fishermen with trawlers. But they were operating in the wrong season. They didn't understand the seasons of God. And a season had just shifted.

The question we must ask is: could any act of worship regardless of the cost be too expensive or costly for our Lord Jesus? The answer is, No.

Jesus describes this anointing as a beautiful thing and highlights the fact that He would not be with disciples in the flesh forever: the act of the woman was a prophetic act of preparation for His burial that would happen not too long from that time.

The reward was outstanding, and no one could have had a more glorious memorial bestowed upon them than Mary of Bethany. Jesus said, "Truly, I say to you, wherever this gospel is proclaimed in the whole world, what she has done will also be told in memory of her." (Matthew 26:13) And even you being reminded about it here is part of the fulfilment of Jesus' prophecy!

Jesus tells about the Last Judgment:

> And the King will answer them, "Truly, I say to you, as you did it to one of the least of these my brothers, you did it to me." Then he will say to those on his left, "Depart from me, you cursed, into the eternal fire prepared for the devil and his angels. For I was hungry and you gave me no food, I was thirsty and you gave me no drink, I was a stranger and you did not welcome me, naked and you did not clothe me, sick and in prison and you did not visit me." Then they also will answer, saying, "Lord, when did we see you hungry or thirsty or a stranger or naked or sick or in prison, and did not minister to you?" Then he will answer them, saying, "Truly, I say to you, as you did not do it to one of the least of these, you did not do it to me." And these will go away into eternal punishment, but the righteous into eternal life. (Matthew 25:40-46)

Our serving of Jesus includes the giving of ourselves and our time to be part of the ongoing work and proclamation of the Gospel.

Giving in any form is an *act of worship* that Jesus acknowledges and rewards.

As marketplace gatekeepers entrusted with money, giving should be our speciality. Our hearts of generosity must be so like the Macedonians! May the Lord show us the best way to give that would have the maximum impact for His kingdom!

The test for the young rich man in the marketplace was not so much about his wealth with God wanting to deprive him of what he had, but rather about having the understanding that the One who provided it for him in the first place was able to provide more in abundance if he was able to let go and give it away for Kingdom purposes.

The rich man lacked one thing, and the only way to get that one thing—a treasure in Heaven—was to give away all he had to the poor and become Jesus's follower. Proverbs 11:24 says,

> One gives freely, yet grows all the richer; another withholds what he should give, and only suffers want.

Job 6:14, Proverbs 3:27 and 11:24 also exhort us not to withhold our generosity. We cannot serve God in the marketplace unless we have an abundance mentality. Most importantly, we must be able to acknowledge the One that gives the power to make wealth. Deuteronomy 8:17-18 says,

> Beware lest you say in your heart, "My power and the might of my hand have gotten me this wealth." You shall remember the Lord your God, for it is he who gives you power to get wealth that he may confirm his covenant that he swore to your fathers, as it is this day.

What is amazing in this passage is that it says that God will confirm His covenant by giving us the power to get wealth! And when we have been blessed, we should never forget that it is because of His covenant and not because of our abilities that we have received His blessings.

Paradoxically, this abundance mentality has very little to do with what we have in our pocket. This often defies our logic and reasoning. God has shown me time and time again during the dry seasons that I needed to learn how to release whatever I have when He is asking me to do so.

Many years ago when, humanly speaking, we were suffering from severe lack, the Lord made a demand which I didn't want to share even with my wife, because I knew I didn't want to hear another opinion or debate on what I was clearly hearing from the Lord. We ran a ministry session after a service on Sunday, and on this day I did not get up to go and minister to those standing in the front, probably because we had very few people and there were enough hands to do the ministry. However, the Lord directed me to a girl in front to hand over my last £10! I obeyed the voice of the Holy Spirit, even when it didn't make sense to part with my last tenner, walked up to the front and handed over the note into her palms.

She began to weep uncontrollably. I gave her a hug, and eventually she stopped crying and left. My only problem was that this last £10 note was meant to buy us the meal for the Sunday afternoon from the supermarket nearby. I had already been looking forward for some rice and chicken!

I hadn't informed my wife that I had given our money away, so once we got into the car, she reminded me that we needed to go shopping. I chose a slightly longer way and when she asked me why I wasn't driving direct to the supermarket, I said that it didn't really matter as long as we got there.

As I was making a turn there was a man knocking on the car window. I opened the window, and the man said that he had been looking for me. He gave me an envelope and left. Both my wife and I wondered what could be inside, as I often get notes outlining a personal problem or a prophetic word from someone.

However, soon the envelope was the last thing on my mind, as I was rehearsing on how to tell my wife I had given away the last £10 meant for our meal. So, I gave it to her while continuing to drive. She opened it, and there was £100 inside! So, we continued the drive to the supermarket and got more than just rice and chicken!

I was able to release what the Lord had given me back into His hands, so that God was able to extend His mercy through me to another child of His that needed £10 even more than I did. I didn't do it because I was expecting Him to bless me or even to replace what I had given away. I simply obeyed, and He provided for me in a way I didn't expect! What I released into His hands came immediately back tenfold!

Proverbs 11:24 says,

> One gives freely, yet grows all the richer; another withholds what he should give, and only suffers want.

EXTREME OBEDIENCE

In Genesis 22:1-19, the Lord instructs Abraham to sacrifice his only son. I don't think that there can be a harder demand to be made on man. This was the ultimate test of obedience. But Abraham trusted the Lord and had the Lord not restrained Abraham that would have been the end of Isaac. But because of Abraham's obedience the Lord knew that there was nothing he would ever withhold from Him. So, He said,

> Do not lay your hand on the boy or do anything to him, for now I know that you fear God, seeing you have not withheld your son, your only son, from me. (Genesis 22:12)

And because of his obedience there now came a greater promise and blessings for Abraham. God gave the kind of promise we would all die for, and these blessings remain with us today long after Abraham. In fact, we are all recipients of Abraham's blessings even though many do not know the cost to Abraham and how much he was willing to sacrifice.

> And the angel of the Lord called unto Abraham out of heaven the second time, and said, By myself have I sworn, saith the Lord, for because thou hast done this thing, and hast not withheld thy son, thine only son: That in blessing I will bless thee, and in multiplying I will multiply thy seed as the stars of the heaven, and as the sand which is upon the sea shore; and thy seed shall possess the gate of his enemies; and in thy seed shall all the nations of the earth be blessed; because thou hast obeyed my voice. So Abraham returned unto his young men, and they rose up and went together to Beersheba; and Abraham dwelt at Beersheba. (Genesis 22:15-19 KJV)

LEARNING TO GIVE ALL

When God asked Abraham to sacrifice Isaac, many other people would have thought that this was the voice of the devil, especially as Isaac was the promised son—there was no way God could have asked Abraham to sacrifice him, anyone could have argued. We can often find plenty of reasonable-sounding arguments as to why not to obey the Lord. But we must learn to obey once we get a prompting from Him. What He asks us to do is not always how we envisage it. But if it is the Lord, the outcome will often far exceed our expectations.

Fortunately, I don't think that this is the kind of testing the Lord would demand of us today. After all, Abraham's faith and Isaac's obedience prophetically foreshadowed the Father's sacrifice and Jesus's obedience, and that sacrifice was once and for all. But at some stage of our walk with God, we will be tested on what we love most.

Philippians 2:8 (ESV) says about the obedience of Jesus:

> And being found in human form, he humbled himself by becoming obedient to the point of death, even death on a cross.

Hebrews 5:8 (ESV) says about Jesus,

> Although he was a son, he learned obedience through what he suffered.

Inheriting the land can take persistent obedience. When there was a famine in the land, God instructed Isaac in Genesis 26 not to leave the country because of God's covenant with Abraham. When we are in a place of famine, we can often think that there is something wrong in the place where we are, and we can decide to depart to a place where the grass seems greener. But we should never disobey the Lord. At times the Lord can instruct us to stay in a place even when, seemingly, our career doesn't seem to be progressing. But God knows the end of a thing before it begins, and there might be a surprise move for you in that place. Obviously, you must be certain that it is God who is asking you to stay and not your fear of change. It is good to share these kinds of dilemmas with prayer partners that can help you to hear God's voice clearly. Sometimes God's purposes aren't immediately obvious, and it can take some time to discern His will.

But Isaiah 46:10 says,

> Declaring the end from the beginning and from ancient times things not yet done, saying, "My counsel shall stand, and I will accomplish all my purpose".

In times like this, our impatience can rob us of our blessing.

Abraham's fruit of obedience was passed on to another generation. Genesis 26:4-5 says,

LEARNING TO GIVE ALL

> I will multiply your offspring as the stars of heaven and will give to your offspring all these lands. And in your offspring all the nations of the earth shall be blessed, because Abraham obeyed my voice and kept my charge, my commandments, my statutes, and my laws.

And another generation would be blessed because of Isaac's obedience.

Genesis 26:12-14 says,

> And Isaac sowed in that land and reaped in the same year a hundredfold. The Lord blessed him, and the man became rich, and gained more and more until he became very wealthy. He had possessions of flocks and herds and many servants, so that the Philistines envied him.

Are you willing to be obedient to the Lord as you serve him in the marketplace? Remember—this was a place of famine. And yet Isaac reaped a hundredfold because he obeyed the Lord. He became wealthy in the land of famine!

The marketplace is a place of serving and stewardship. Your purpose is not to serve money but to steward it on behalf of the Lord.

WHAT IS STEWARDSHIP?
1 Corinthians 4:2 says,

> Moreover, it is required of stewards that they be found faithful.

Stewardship is faithfulness in operation. It means you operate at the highest level of integrity and use the resources the Lord has placed in your hands to the glory of His name. And it is easier to remain obedient and manage the resources well when you see yourself as the steward and not the owner.

Faithfulness is a key requirement in serving the Lord in the marketplace. Jesus says,

> One who is faithful in a very little is also faithful in much, and one who is dishonest in a very little is also dishonest in much. (Luke 16:10)

You must be above reproach, not arrogant or quick-tempered and especially not greedy for gain. Greed has ruined many in the world of business; it is a trap that those in the marketplace as gatekeepers must never fall into. The Word of God shows we can fall so easily, no matter who we are, but thankfully it also gives us practical guidance of how to avoid failure.

LEARNING TO GIVE ALL

ASK YOURSELF THESE QUESTIONS

1. Are you going to withhold from others what He has given to you?
2. Are you going to give excuses and pretend to be a good steward when you are not?
3. Will you be the first person to answer the call when it comes to giving to the work of the Kingdom?

—⚜—

How could you worship two gods at the same time? You will have to hate one and love the other, or be devoted to one and despise the other. You can't worship the true God while enslaved to the god of money! (Matthew 6:24 TPT)

—⚜—

CHAPTER 4
RENDER TO CAESAR THE THINGS THAT ARE CAESAR'S

> Jesus said to them, "Render to Caesar the things that are Caesar's, and to God the things that are God's." And they marveled at him. (Mark 12:17)

There are two sides of the coin to Jesus's command to give to God what belongs to God and to man what belongs to man, and both are indispensable.

GOD AND CAESARS

The Jewish leaders wanted to entrap Jesus, as He had just told them the Parable of the Tenants, and how they had rejected Jesus, the cornerstone. So, they sent some to catch Him in His words. They asked:

> "Is it lawful for us to give tribute to Caesar, or not?" But he perceived their craftiness, and said to them,

> "Show me a denarius. Whose likeness and inscription does it have?" They said, "Caesar's." He said to them, "Then render to Caesar the things that are Caesar's, and to God the things that are God's." (Luke 20:20-25)

The denarius had the Roman emperor's image, and it represented the tribute they were supposed to give to him. But giving taxes to the Roman Empire wasn't a popular position in the 1st century Judea. Taxes were a volatile issue in Israel. All of Rome's subjects, including the people of Israel, laboured under the empire's heavy taxation. Many Jews believed that paying any tax to pagan rulers contradicted God's lordship over his people. On the other hand, encouraging the Jews not to pay taxes would have been considered rebellious by the Roman occupying forces. So, the Jewish leaders had Jesus where they wanted: if Jesus said that it was fine to pay taxes, he would become unpopular with the people, if He said that the people didn't need to pay taxes, He could be arrested. But Jesus sidestepped their question and took an opportunity to expose their idolatry.

According to Jesus, people should give to God that which bears his image and likeness, namely, themselves. As man is the image of God, he belongs to God fully.

The coin was a representation of one the Romans venerated and that was Caesar. In those days, the emperor cult was slowly taking form, and Caesar was becoming like god to the Romans. His image was on the coin, so it belonged to him.

On the opposite side of the coin was a picture of the Roman goddess of peace, Pax, with the Latin inscription of the "High Priest." Even if all Romans didn't believe in the divinity of the emperor, they all certainly believed that the Roman Empire represented by Caesar was the major instrument in the hands of their gods.

But who is our High Priest? These images on the coin contradict everything we are taught in the Scripture about the lordship of Jesus over our lives. He is the true God and our High Priest, so any other high priest is a high priest of idolatry. And the Jews had their own high priest over the temple in Jerusalem, and yet they were trying to trap Jesus with a coin that represented a completely different religious system. The Jewish leaders were completely focused on the idea that paying taxes to an authority that didn't believe in their God but in other gods was wrong, so much so, that they had forgotten to look at whose image was on the coin.

Worshipping the Roman gods was considered idolatry, but the Jewish leaders seemed more than happy to keep the money that honoured the Roman gods. So, Jesus simply pointed to their hypocrisy and idolatry of money. As far as Jesus was concerned, anyone focusing on money rather than focusing on giving the image of God back to God was missing the point!

But this wasn't just a cunning answer to a trick question. Jesus also pointed to an important principle. No matter how godly or ungodly we perceive our governments to be, we are still commanded to pay the taxes to them. The apostle Paul says in Romans 13:6-7:

> For because of this you also pay taxes, for the authorities are ministers of God, attending to this very thing. Pay to all what is owed to them: taxes to whom taxes are owed, revenue to whom revenue is owed, respect to whom respect is owed, honor to whom honor is owed.

Some of Jesus' disciples started as tax collectors: Thomas, Matthew and Levi. And Levi had a great party in his house with Jesus and many tax collectors.

> And Levi made him a great feast in his house, and there was a large company of tax collectors and others reclining at table with them. (Luke 5:29)

Jesus' friendship with tax collectors was probably the reason why the Jews asked Him about the taxes in the first place. But Jesus had come for everyone regardless of their occupation. So, perhaps Jesus's position on taxes wasn't very clear. But in this instance, He managed to clarify it, probably to the dissatisfaction of many of His listeners.

This is often a sore point especially for those in the marketplace with good earnings. Those that are in the marketplace often think that the government is demanding too much of their hard-earned money as income tax.

Depending on the nation where you are residing in for tax purposes, tax rate could be as high as 50%—or even more. In time of writing, for the UK it is:

UK basic tax rate
20% on annual earnings above the PAYE tax threshold and up to £34,500

UK higher tax rate
40% on annual earnings from £34,501 to £150,000

UK additional tax rate
45% on annual earnings above £150,000

I would imagine that some of us reading this book might fall in the region of the 45%.

How much more will you feel that you are being taxed if you are running your own business! And that is the area where I believe the Lord is calling many of the marketplace gatekeepers: to become an entrepreneur rather than an employee.

But no matter how disgruntled you feel about taxes, we have the guidance from our Heavenly Tax Adviser, and it is that we should owe no one. This is the example we must follow.

But this wasn't the only time Jesus encountered taxes in the Gospel stories. At another time, Jesus was asked to pay the temple tax—this time to the Jewish authorities.

> When they came to Capernaum, the collectors of the two-drachma tax went up to Peter and said, "Does your teacher not pay the tax?" He said, "Yes." And when he came into the house, Jesus spoke to him first, saying, "What do you think, Simon? From whom do kings of the earth take toll or tax? From their sons or from others?" And when he said, "From others," Jesus said to him, "Then the sons are free. However, not to give offense to them, go to the sea and cast a hook and take the first fish that comes up, and when you open its mouth you will find a shekel. Take that and give it to them for me and for yourself." (Matthew 17:24-27)

We do not only have to pay the taxes but the correct taxes without fiddling with the figures! Declare the right amount, take whatever allowance is due to you and warn your auditors not to give you more than you are lawfully entitled to.

RENDER TO CAESAR THE THINGS THAT ARE CAESAR'S

ANANIAS AND SAPPHIRA

The story of Ananias and Sapphira is a warning example about what can happen when we don't make an honest declaration about our finances—especially when it comes to the Lord.

> But a man named Ananias, with his wife Sapphira, sold a piece of property, and with his wife's knowledge he kept back for himself some of the proceeds and brought only a part of it and laid it at the apostles' feet. But Peter said, "Ananias, why has Satan filled your heart to lie to the Holy Spirit and to keep back for yourself part of the proceeds of the land? While it remained unsold, did it not remain your own? And after it was sold, was it not at your disposal? Why is it that you have contrived this deed in your heart? You have not lied to man but to God." When Ananias heard these words, he fell down and breathed his last. And great fear came upon all who heard of it. (Acts 5:1-5)

This is one of the most shocking stories in the Bible, and definitely an unexpected twist in the birth story of the Early Church. We have just learned that Jesus has died for the sins of all, and then a man falls down dead because of undeclared earnings! And what follows is equally shocking.

> After an interval of about three hours his wife came in, not knowing what had happened. And Peter

said to her, "Tell me whether you sold the land for so much." And she said, "Yes, for so much." But Peter said to her, "How is it that you have agreed together to test the Spirit of the Lord? Behold, the feet of those who have buried your husband are at the door, and they will carry you out." Immediately she fell down at his feet and breathed her last. When the young men came in they found her dead, and they carried her out and buried her beside her husband. And great fear came upon the whole church and upon all who heard of these things. (Acts 5:7-11)

Sometimes I wonder what would follow if that happened in church today. It would certainly be a wake-up call for us as believers but especially for us the gatekeepers in the marketplace. It is important to render to God what belongs to Him, and if we pledge to give Him something, that promise can become binding in His eyes.

TITHE AND OFFERINGS

Our offerings to the Lord are based on our free choice. You can give as much or as little as you want. It is good to give not just to the church but also to the poor, the widows and the orphans. It is good to give to charitable causes and find a Kingdom cause that you support out of your income.

Giving tithes has caused so much controversy in the last couple of years and many are challenging the using of Malachi 3:10 to teach about tithing.

RENDER TO CAESAR THE THINGS THAT ARE CAESAR'S

Personally, I believe that this teaching is still a sound biblical principle even in the Church, but there is a diversity of views on this issue. But whatever your stand, there are many Christians that are giving well over the 10% that we call tithe to their local church.

When we give our tithes to a local church, we are helping to build the Kingdom of God, we are helping to build the house of God and the church to function while the church ministers get on with their work of helping the people without having to spend most of their time worrying about how to pay the bills linked to ministry. My view is that we shouldn't be too focused on how the church leadership spends this money, unless there are clear wrongdoings. Many have stopped giving to the local church because they disagree with how the church budget is spent. But God is the ultimate judge of all, and only He knows the true motivations of each person's heart.

I do not want to make light of the fact that this process has been abused by many leaders over the years. But my teaching on giving for the marketplace gatekeepers is on a different level. Romans 12:8 refers to giving as one of the spiritual gifts and exhorts anyone with this gift to give generously. It is about giving till it hurts and knowing that the one who made you to be a steward is able to supply you more abundantly than you can ever imagine!

MARKETPLACE GATEKEEPERS

Paul writes in 2 Corinthians 8:1-5:

> We want you to know, brothers, about the grace of God that has been given among the churches of Macedonia, for in a severe test of affliction, their abundance of joy and their extreme poverty have overflowed in a wealth of generosity on their part. For they gave according to their means, as I can testify, and beyond their means, of their own accord, begging us earnestly for the favor of taking part in the relief of the saints—and this, not as we expected, but they gave themselves first to the Lord and then by the will of God to us.

The churches in Macedonia had an abundance mentality in their approach to giving.

Paul adds in the same letter:

> But this *I say*: He who sows sparingly will also reap sparingly, and he who sows bountifully will also reap bountifully. (2 Corinthians 9:6)

I believe this Bible verse is applicable especially to marketplace gatekeepers. The truth is you can never out-give God, but your giving will certainly be commensurate with your blessing, as promised in the Bible. As a marketplace gatekeeper you don't want to give God your crumbs, but you want to give to the Lord the best of your substance! You must remember that you are a steward rather than the owner.

RENDER TO CAESAR THE THINGS THAT ARE CAESAR'S

Haggai 2:8 says, "The silver is mine, and the gold is mine, declares the Lord of hosts." Psalm 50:10 adds, "For every beast of the forest is mine, the cattle on a thousand hills."

The Macedonian church gave over and beyond, and that should be our example—whether you believe in tithing or not. The teaching of Paul should be more than sufficient regarding to giving for us as believers and certainly as marketplace gatekeepers. Not every Christian has been given the gift of giving to the same degree, but if you have been called to operate with finances, then generosity is the only way to operate in godly way.

We must give with ecstatic joy and an abundant mentality, trusting that the same God is able to bless us far beyond our expectations. This is intentional, and we don't give to receive, but we will always receive, because God promises it.

In Luke 6:38 Jesus says,

> Give, and it will be given to you. Good measure, pressed down, shaken together, running over, will be put into your lap. For with the measure you use it will be measured back to you.

Do you believe this? God is a giver, and we must learn to be extravagant givers as His children.

God is the supreme head over your life, but God has prepared someone to help you along the way, advise and encourage you. These people are your destiny helpers, and you have also been called to be someone else's destiny helper. Find your helper!

CHAPTER 5
FAVOUR HAS A PURPOSE

You must have heard the saying that when life gives you lemons, make lemonade. The truth is that life doesn't seem to treat everyone the same way, and sometimes you don't even get lemons to make that lemonade.

Some seem to go through their lives in a bubble of favour without ever experiencing any major misfortunes. And they always seem to have plenty. Others go through life without any idea where the next meal will come from and without a penny in their pocket to take a bus to the next job interview.

I have seen many days when I haven't had a penny, so I can empathise with the poor! But God has also opened the door to palaces for me, and I know that the lot of the rich isn't always as glamorous as it might seem. Even those who never seem to receive lemons can have a hidden cupboard of them in their lives!

MARKETPLACE GATEKEEPERS

However, those that I am addressing here are the ones that have been fortunate enough to be in a position that might have once seemed unreachable for them. You know that even though you have worked hard, there is no way that you could be holding the position you have now had it not been by divine providence!

Being an excellent employee is not always the determining factor for getting a promotion. There are many other factors that could be at play. If you come from the ethnic minorities, it can be doubly as hard to get that promotion, even with government-instituted non-discrimination policies. Governments are unable to monitor their non-discrimination policies effectively, and only the most flagrant violations, which often lead to litigation, are caught. And even if a company is sued for discrimination and loses the case, discrimination will often just continue but will only be concealed more effectively.

In some organisations the people of a certain race can never rise above a certain grade, their expertise notwithstanding. Or if they do, they might find out that the real power seems to escape them, no matter how high their apparent position might be.

There is also plenty of sexual discrimination against women. This is being addressed to some degree, and we can see more female executives rising to the position of directors and CEOs—but often with less pay! But generally, if you are a female CEO from an ethnic minority, you must be exceptionally good in what you are doing, and there won't have been any old boy networks to help you on the way. But the exceptional is not the norm, and we should not be misled by some front cover feature stories made of the exceptions.

However, whether you are there against all the odds or the odds were on your side, you are where you are for a reason. When you have a good look around, and you know without a shadow of doubt that there were others who are more qualified, and yet you have been chosen, then you know that it is God's favour that has taken you there. When you know the daily obstacles that you are facing and the hard times you have come through, you know that it is God's favour that has taken you there. But the purpose is not that you are there, the purpose is what you will do there!

Ruth and Esther are two incredible women in the Bible. They started from a low position, but the Lord's favour was upon them so strongly that they ended up shaping the future. It wasn't because they were smarter or better than the rest, but God chose them to show forth His glory and power through them. We must understand that when similar favour comes to us, it is not so much for us but for God's purposes to be outplayed through the simple and the outcast.

RUTH

The story of Ruth begins with Naomi who is Ruth's mother-in-law. She was originally from Bethlehem but relocated to the land of Moab because of famine. Naomi's sons married in the land of Moab. However, Naomi lost her husband and her two sons, which was a tragic thing to happen to someone who moved to another country in search for a better life. Many of us can identify with Naomi and her husband Elimelech, as many of us have also immigrated to other nations to better our lives and offer a better life to our families. But no one expects to lose members of their families in that process!

After losing all the blood family members Naomi planned to make a return to Bethlehem alone, as the famine had subsided. She wasn't planning on returning with her daughters-in-law, as she preferred them to remarry because they had no children. As she loved them, she thought it would be best for them to stay in their country. Ruth 1:8 says,

> But Naomi said to her two daughters-in-law, "Go, return each of you to her mother's house. May the Lord deal kindly with you, as you have dealt with the dead and with me."

However, despite her insistence Ruth, one of the two daughters-in-law, refused to leave Naomi and insisted to follow her despite the risk of never getting another husband. After all, she was a Moabite and Naomi a Jew, and no law-obeying Jew would marry a foreigner. Ruth 1:16 says,

> But Ruth said, "Do not urge me to leave you or to return from following you. For where you go I will go, and where you lodge I will lodge. Your people shall be my people, and your God my God."

So, they both went to Bethlehem, and they were warmly welcomed by the relatives. But Naomi was sorrowful, as she had come back empty-handed with nothing to show for her sojourn to the land of Moab. Perhaps you can identify with this, and are scared to ever return to the land of your birth, because you feel that you have not accomplished much to show that it was worthwhile for you to have left in the first place!

However, if God so directs, we should never be afraid if we have to return, as there could be a God-given opportunity waiting for us!

Genesis 31:3 says,

> Then the Lord said to Jacob, "Return to the land of your fathers and to your kindred, and I will be with you."

There was a time when the Lord commanded Jacob to return to the land of his father, even though the

Lord had prospered him where he was with his uncle Laban. But his time was up according to God's timing. Jacob had prospered despite the jealousy and envy, and his uncle had been a harsh taskmaster. In Genesis 31:6-7 Jacob says to his wives Rachel and Leah,

> You know that I have served your father with all my strength, yet your father has cheated me and changed my wages ten times. But God did not permit him to harm me.

But even if your boss is cheating you of your wages, God sees it! And it seems that no matter how many times Laban tried to cheat Jacob, he could never cheat him of God's blessing. But unlike Jacob, Naomi seemed to be returning after having been robbed of her greatest blessings—her husband and sons. Ruth 1:22 says,

> So Naomi returned, and Ruth the Moabite her daughter-in-law with her, who returned from the country of Moab. And they came to Bethlehem at the beginning of barley harvest.

Sometimes the Lord providentially arranges our lives in ways that we cannot fathom. I know many that have taken the steps to return without anything to show for their sojourn abroad. And this has turned out to be one of the best decisions of their lives, as it has turned out that the Lord had been waiting for them to return!

When we receive the prompting of the Lord, we must act. This prompting can be a quiet voice in your heart, or it could be someone else exhorting you. 2 Corinthians 13:1 says,

> By the mouth of two or three witnesses every word shall be established.

But the timing must be right.

For Ruth and Naomi, returning in the time of barley harvest was fortunate. Ruth did not waste any more time; she immediately started to look for work. And what better place to work than in the fields of Boaz who was a relative of Naomi's late husband!

Boaz had heard how Ruth had remained faithful to her mother-in-law. This also demonstrated that she had forsaken the gods of Moab and embraced the God of Israel. He was willing to give her a job to work in his fields.

Ruth 2:10 says,

> Then she fell on her face, bowing to the ground, and said to him, "Why have I found favor in your eyes, that you should take notice of me, since I am a foreigner?"

A little later in the story, Ruth 2:15-16 tells,

> When she rose to glean, Boaz instructed his young men, saying, "Let her glean even among the sheaves, and do not reproach her. And also pull out some from the bundles for her and leave it for her to glean, and do not rebuke her."

She had found favour already, as Boaz instructed his men to drop some of the harvest on purpose! So, Ruth didn't exactly do all the hard work of gleaning.

But Naomi was still thinking of Ruth's future wellbeing and wanted her to be married, but to a relative, as was customary. And Boaz seemed like a very suitable candidate, especially as Boaz was her kinsman redeemer, a male relative who, according to various laws found in the Pentateuch, had the privilege or responsibility to act for a relative who was in trouble, danger, or need of vindication. So, Naomi instructed Ruth on how to approach him.

> Wash therefore and anoint yourself, and put on your cloak and go down to the threshing floor, but do not make yourself known to the man until he has finished eating and drinking. (Ruth 3:3)

Prophetically, there is a lot going on here, as God is Israel's Redeemer, and Boaz foreshadows Christ in the salvation story. Ruth 2:20 says,

> And Naomi said to her daughter-in-law, "May he be blessed by the Lord, whose kindness has not forsaken

the living or the dead!" Naomi also said to her, "The man is a close relative of ours, one of our redeemers."

Naomi was certainly hopeful about Boaz, and she was ready to follow this hope up in a very practical way. Sometimes we need the help of someone to push us into our destiny. Be watchful in this regard as a marketplace gatekeeper!

So, Naomi was busy matchmaking and instructing her daughter-in-law on how to behave and what to say. Ruth listened to all her instructions. We must always have mentors in our lives: people who know more than us and are willing to give good advice. Ruth carried out all her instructions, Boaz granted her wishes, and the rest is history.

Boaz says to Ruth in Ruth 3:11,

> And now, my daughter, do not fear. I will do for you all that you ask, for all my fellow townsmen know that you are a worthy woman.

Ruth was a worthy woman. The good testimony of her life came now to bless her. Likewise, there are many moments in our lives when only a good testimony can help us move to the next level, but a bad testimony will obstruct us.

The problem was that Boaz was not the closest male to Naomi in the family. There was someone else who was even closer, and this person had the right and the responsibility to be the kinsman redeemer. It was obvious that Boaz loved Ruth but raising the issue of the kinsman redeemer also raised the possibility that Ruth would be married to another man. Perhaps that was the reason Boaz had delayed raising the issue himself. Ruth 4:1 says,

> Now Boaz had gone up to the gate and sat down there. And behold, the redeemer, of whom Boaz had spoken, came by. So Boaz said, "Turn aside, friend; sit down here." And he turned aside and sat down.

This man wanted Naomi's land but when he finds out that he needs to marry Ruth as part of the deal, he refuses. It tells of Naomi's love for Ruth that she is willing to let go of the land she owns to help Ruth get married. It turns out that she's not just a *mentor* but also an *investor*.

Then Boaz went to the gate to redeem Ruth. It is important to note that such transactions take place at the gates. In the Old Testament times, gates were the place where decisions were made and agreements completed. Today, corporate headquarters of companies and institutions have replaced these ancient, physical gates as the places where important decisions are made.

Ruth 4:9-11 says,

FAVOUR HAS A PURPOSE

Then Boaz said to the elders and all the people, "You are witnesses this day that I have bought from the hand of Naomi all that belonged to Elimelech and all that belonged to Chilion and to Mahlon. Also Ruth the Moabite, the widow of Mahlon, I have bought to be my wife, to perpetuate the name of the dead in his inheritance that the name of the dead may not be cut off from among his brothers and from the gate of his native place. You are witnesses this day." Then all the people who were at the gate and the elders said, "We are witnesses. May the Lord make the woman, who is coming into your house, like Rachel and Leah, who together built up the house of Israel. May you act worthily in Ephrathah and be renowned in Bethlehem."

Then she married Ruth without any further delays. Ruth 4:13 says,

> So Boaz took Ruth, and she became his wife. And he went in to her, and the Lord gave her conception, and she bore a son.

Ruth's son Obed was the father of Jesse, the father of David. This foreign woman gives birth to a royal dynasty! The favour of the Lord was upon her to fulfil her destiny. Everything was against her, but she was able to enter God's purposes because of His favour. And Ruth was one of the women mentioned in the genealogy of Jesus!

How amazing is this? From a widow to the great-grandmother of King David! If that is not favour, then what is?

QUEEN ESTHER

Esther was known as Hadassah by her Jewish name and heritage. She was brought up by her uncle Mordecai in a strange land of Persia where they were complete outsiders. But then the reigning queen was banished from ever appearing before the king because she declined the invitation of the king to the banquet.

A new queen had to be sought for the king, and all the beautiful women in the nation were selected. Esther was one of them.

At Mordecai's advice, Esther did not disclose her identity as a Jew, as this could have disqualified her.

Esther 2:7-8 says about Mordecai:

> He was bringing up Hadassah, that is Esther, the daughter of his uncle, for she had neither father nor mother. The young woman had a beautiful figure and was lovely to look at, and when her father and her mother died, Mordecai took her as his own daughter. So when the king's order and his edict were proclaimed, and when many young women were gathered in Susa the citadel in custody of Hegai, Esther also was taken into the king's palace and put in custody of Hegai, who had charge of the women.

FAVOUR HAS A PURPOSE

Mordechai kept a close watch to make sure all was well with Esther, walking past the court of the harem every day to find out what was happening to her.

Many other women soon got distracted by the perfumes and the jewellery that were available in the court, and they forgot the reason for being there in the first place. In the harem Esther found a mentor by the name of Hegai, the king's eunuch, who told her what to do. Her Uncle Mordecai had been her mentor until now, but the situation had changed, and this was a totally different environment. Mordecai had no idea about what was going in the harem, as the king's eunuchs were the only males allowed in.

Here we learn that one mentor might not be able to counsel us in every area of life. Esther 1:15 tells,

> When the turn came for Esther the daughter of Abihail the uncle of Mordecai, who had taken her as his own daughter, to go in to the king, she asked for nothing except what Hegai the king's eunuch, who had charge of the women, advised. Now Esther was winning favor in the eyes of all who saw her.

Esther 2:17 says that

> the king loved Esther more than all the women, and she won grace and favor in his sight more than all the virgins." He set the royal crown on her head and made her queen instead of Vashti.

Esther took the advice of her new mentor, and she did all that she was told and won the favour of the king.

Now, most of us would have praised God and thought that the ultimate purpose of God to make Esther the Queen was now accomplished. Yet God never promotes someone merely for the sake of promotion, but He always has a bigger plan that will involve helping other people. When God positions us for a blessing, He does so that He would also be able to bless others through us as well.

There was an evil plot by Haman, the king's vizier, to annihilate all the Jews in the land. This plan was activated because Mordecai refused to kneel in front of Haman, and Haman discovered that Mordecai was a Jew. All the king's officials knelt in front of Haman at the king's gate. Mordecai didn't. Enraged, through cunning, Haman gets the king to give him permission to kill all the Jews in the Persian Empire.

We can see here how there is a fierce battle over who is honoured at the gates, and that when the gates of power are in the control of idolaters, it can be very harmful for the people of God. We can see that ultimately the question of who controls the gates can be a life-and-death issue.

Esther had to be reminded by her uncle and mentor Mordecai that the reason for her promotion was to bring deliverance to her people, the Jews. Sometimes we get so comfortable with our new position or elevation that we forget why we are there in the first place, and unless we recognise that it wasn't because we were the best or the smartest, but by God's divine providence, we can easily miss our purpose.

Esther 4:13-14 says,

> Then Mordecai told them to reply to Esther, "Do not think to yourself that in the king's palace you will escape any more than all the other Jews. For if you keep silent at this time, relief and deliverance will rise for the Jews from another place, but you and your father's house will perish. *And who knows whether you have not come to the kingdom for such a time as this?*"

Esther rises to the challenge and puts all her plans in place to stop this evil plot by Haman. She is willing to lay her life on the line.

In Esther 4:16 she says to Mordecai,

> Go, gather all the Jews to be found in Susa, and hold a fast on my behalf, and do not eat or drink for three days, night or day. I and my young women will also fast as you do. Then I will go to the king, though it is against the law, and if I perish, I perish.

She takes the risk and appears before the king without an appointment. Fortunately, the King raises his sceptre and Esther has favour and is safe to come before the king, who seems delighted of her presence, so much so that he is willing to grant her any wish. But rather than asking for anything directly, she invites the king and Haman to the banquet she has prepared.

Esther 5:6 tells about the first banquet:

> And as they were drinking wine after the feast, the king said to Esther, "What is your wish? It shall be granted you. And what is your request? Even to the half of my kingdom, it shall be fulfilled."

Haman was the special guest of honour at this royal banquet, and he was very pleased about it. Obviously, he had no idea that Esther also was a Jew. Psalm 23:5 says, "You prepare a table before me in the presence of my enemies; you anoint my head with oil; my cup overflows." So often, if you operate in the marketplace, God will lead you to situations where your enemies dine next to you!

Instead of making her request, Esther asks him to attend a second feast.

Esther 7:1-6 says,

> So the king and Haman went in to feast with Queen Esther. And on the second day, as they were drinking wine after the feast, the king again said to Esther, "What is your wish, Queen Esther? It shall be granted you. And what is your request? Even to the half of my kingdom, it shall be fulfilled." Then Queen Esther answered, "If I have found favor in your sight, O king, and if it please the king, let my life be granted me for my wish, and my people for my request. For we

have been sold, I and my people, to be destroyed, to be killed, and to be annihilated. If we had been sold merely as slaves, men and women, I would have been silent, for our affliction is not to be compared with the loss to the king." Then King Ahasuerus said to Queen Esther, "Who is he, and where is he, who has dared to do this?" And Esther said, "A foe and enemy! This wicked Haman!" Then Haman was terrified before the king and the queen.

Haman is hanged in the gallows he had prepared for Esther's Uncle Mordecai, a Jew who sits daily at the King's Gate and is his arch enemy.

But the king's order to kill the Jews had already been published, and it could not be revoked according to Persian law of the day.

In Esther 8:8 Esther speaks to the king about giving the Jews the right to defend themselves as a solution.

> But you may write as you please with regard to the Jews, in the name of the king, and seal it with the king's ring, for an edict written in the name of the king and sealed with the king's ring cannot be revoked.

Esther 8:13 says,

> A copy of what was written was to be issued as a decree in every province, being publicly displayed to all peoples, and the Jews were to be ready on that day to take vengeance on their enemies.

With the new decree, the Jews were now able to defend themselves against any attack, and there was deliverance for the Jews in the land of Persia. Esther 8:16-17 says that because of the king's edict many people in Persia declared themselves Jews, as the fear of the Jews had fallen on them. Perhaps they realised that if they would obey the first edict devised by Haman, they would probably end up dead, because the second edict showed where the king's favour really rested.

LESSONS FROM RUTH AND ESTHER

Both Ruth and Esther found themselves in positions far higher than the position granted to them by people because God's favour was upon them.

Ruth became part of the lineage of Jesus by being faithful and loyal not only to her mother-in-law Naomi—having lost her husband she had hung on to Naomi—but also to the true God of Israel, abandoning idolatry and any other gods of her family heritage. She found favour with God, and she was not despised even when she was a foreigner in the land of the Jews. There was a great purpose behind her new position, which she reached by listening to her mentor on how to go about things.

The king offered half of his kingdom to Esther, which would have made her extremely powerful. But she wasn't making a request for herself but for her people. But that necessitated her revealing that she was also a Jew, which was risky for her.

However, she was constantly reminded by her uncle and mentor why she had been promoted. He pushed her to the place of prominence by putting her forward as a prospective queen amongst the other virgins in the land. Esther also paid special attention to another mentor by the name of Hegai in the king's harem.

Do you have a good mentor that can help you find promotion, find the right direction and remind you of your purpose and destiny? If you operate in the marketplace, your mentor doesn't necessarily have to be a Christian. Pray to get a mentor in your workplace, and if you run your own business, pray that God will help you find a person with the necessary experience to help you navigate the waters in the marketplace.

There are sharks in the marketplace, and if you are not surefooted, the sharks can eat your business alive and cut your aspirations short. Ultimately, God is the supreme head over your life, but He has prepared someone to help you along the way, advise and encourage you.

These people are your destiny helpers, and you have also been called to be someone else's destiny helper. Timothy had Paul to help and mentor him, and this brought a major change in his life. Church tradition tells us that Timothy became the first bishop of the church in Ephesus, where he mentored many others.

Paul writes in 1 Timothy 1:2,

> To Timothy, my true child in the faith: Grace, mercy, and peace from God the Father and Christ Jesus our Lord.

He writes 1 Timothy 1:18,

> This charge I entrust to you, Timothy, my child, in accordance with the prophecies previously made about you, that by them you may wage the good warfare.

He writes in 1 Timothy 4:15-16,

> Practice these things, immerse yourself in them, so that all may see your progress. Keep a close watch on yourself and on the teaching. Persist in this, for by so doing you will save both yourself and your hearers.

He writes in 1 Timothy 6:12,

> Fight the good fight of the faith. Take hold of the eternal life to which you were called and about which you made the good confession in the presence of many witnesses.

How would you feel today if Paul offered to be your

mentor? You would grab that offer with both hands. But that is what he is doing through his letters!

We can see the pattern of their relationship through Paul's letters. Paul was always there to guide Timothy, and he can guide you too through his words in the Bible.

As a marketplace gatekeeper you must have an awareness of the fact that where you are is where you should be, and you need to find purpose in that place. This purpose could be:

- To be a light in the workplace
- To be a witness of Christ everywhere through your actions
- To be a treasurer for the Kingdom by giving to God's work, charities, to alleviate poverty, and so on.

These are but just a few examples and by no means an exhaustive list. The purposes for favour would differ for each person.

So, never forget that favour has a purpose. Esther 4:14 says,

> For if you keep silent at this time, relief and deliverance will rise for the Jews from another place, but you and your father's house will perish. And who knows whether you have not come to the kingdom for such a time as this?

The process of receiving begins with thanksgiving, and we keep on thanking Him until we receive. And we also keep on thanking even when we don't receive.

CHAPTER 6
THANKSGIVING BRINGS MULTIPLICATION

> Oh give thanks to the Lord, for he is good, for his steadfast love endures forever! (Psalm 107:1 ESV)

An essential ingredient for multiplication and receiving God's blessing over our lives is the heart of thanksgiving. A thankful heart is a heart that appreciates God's mercy and God's provision.

You are where you are by the grace of God. I commend you for your diligence and hard work and would never minimise this, but it is by the grace of God! We ought to be thankful and show it in our regular praise and thanksgiving to the Giver, who has kept us and is still able to keep us.

We are all familiar with the story of Jesus feeding five thousand men with five loaves of bread and two fish. As the women and the children were not counted, there might have been as many as ten thousand people there.

Mark 6:34-38 says,

> When he went ashore he saw a great crowd, and he had compassion on them, because they were like sheep without a shepherd. And he began to teach them many things. And when it grew late, his disciples came to him and said, "This is a desolate place, and the hour is now late. Send them away to go into the surrounding countryside and villages and buy themselves something to eat." But he answered them, "You give them something to eat." And they said to him, "Shall we go and buy two hundred denarii worth of bread and give it to them to eat?" And he said to them, "How many loaves do you have? Go and see." And when they had found out, they said, "Five, and two fish."

The disciples must have been aware about the people's predicament hence they were quick to let Jesus know that He needed to send them away, as there was no supply or sustenance for the large crowd that was before them.

But Jesus seemed unperturbed by the situation and asked the people to sit down orderly, so the seemingly non-existing food could be distributed. I don't want to imagine what went on in the minds of the disciples as they carried out the instruction of the Rabbi!

But Jesus was ready to use the seemingly small things to perform the miraculous through the giving of thanks. Don't wait until you become a millionaire

THANKSGIVING BRINGS MULTIPLICATION

to give thanks! Give thanks with the little in your hands, so He can multiply it.

Then Jesus took the five loaves of bread and the two fish from them. He said a simple and short prayer of thanksgiving to His Father in heaven and blessed what He had in His hands. Then He gave it to His disciples who in turn distributed these to the multitudes who were already seated.

Why did He give the food back to His disciples? Had he already multiplied the fish and bread, and they now had to be distributed? No. It seems that the food was being multiplied whilst in the hands of the disciples.

What the Lord wants to give out to the world is already in your hands! He wants you to give him thanks for it and bless it, so He can multiply it for you to distribute to the needy, to the poor, to orphans and widows.

God is always in the business of multiplying whatever He gives us, as we become thankful and do not take it for granted.

THANKSGIVING GIVES ACCESS TO MIRACLES

Colossians 3:17 says,

> And whatever you do, in word or deed, do everything in the name of the Lord Jesus, giving thanks to God the Father through him.

One of my favourite verses in the Bible is 1 Thessalonians 5:16-18, which says,

> Rejoice always, pray without ceasing, give thanks in all circumstances; for this is the will of God in Christ Jesus for you.

The whole essence of a Christian life is captured in these verses. This is what the life of a Christian should be!

But rejoicing always, how is it possible? It means the circumstances of your life are not the determining factor of your consistent and fervent worship and thankfulness to God. Read Psalm 139 if you want to really understand this.

God knows about everything that is happening to you. Nothing happens to you without His permission, and unlike what most Christians would like to believe, it's not always the devil that is behind our difficulties. We give too much credit to the devil for everything that goes wrong, but if it's the devil, the Lord is allowing it, so we can grow in our walk of faith with Him.

David was always able to give thanks. Most of the psalms are full of thanksgiving. And by far one of the most popular one is Psalm 100:4, which says,

> Enter his gates with *thanksgiving* and his courts with praise; give thanks to him and praise his name. (NIV)

THANKSGIVING BRINGS MULTIPLICATION

Psalms 69:30 says,

> I will praise God's name in song and glorify him with *thanksgiving*. (NIV)

Psalm 95:2 says,

> Let us come before him with *thanksgiving* and extol him with music and song. (NIV)

Giving thanks brings a multiplier effect if we apply it to every situation.

As you can see from these verses, David knew the only way to his successes was through the giving of thanks.

So, come into His presence, praising Him with songs and glorifying God, and approach God always with thanksgiving!

Thanksgiving should never be dependent on your feelings or whether your bills have been paid but on the knowledge that the Lord is always good, no matter how you feel. Psalm 50:14 says,

> Offer to God a sacrifice of *thanksgiving*, and perform your vows to the Most High.

Psalms 50:23 says,

> The one who offers thanksgiving as his sacrifice glorifies me; to one who orders his way rightly I will show the salvation of God!

The Lord sees your thanksgiving as a sacrifice—but most of us only give thanks after we have received something and not before. This is where our mind-set needs to be transformed, because only the one who has faith will thank for something before he or she has received it.

We are taught from a very young age that when someone gives us something, we must show some appreciation. Often our parents ask us if we have said thank you, and we are made to make amends as soon as possible if we haven't done so. What we have never been taught is how to say thank you before we have received! You can't possibly teach that to a very young child, and even many adults would probably not accept that you would need to say thank you to anyone before you have received anything from them.

But the ways of the Spirit go often against the grain. They defy logic.

The ESV version of Psalm 50:23 implies that thanksgiving leads to man ordering "his way rightly", which will lead to salvation. In order to receive anything from God we must often begin with an offering of praise and thanksgiving.

THANKSGIVING BRINGS MULTIPLICATION

We have to renew our understanding and as gatekeepers and potential Kingdom treasurers begin to apply the spiritual principle that in order to receive anything from the Lord, we must thank Him in advance and praise Him.

The process of receiving begins with thanksgiving, and we keep on thanking Him until we receive. And we keep on thanking even when we don't receive. It can be hard to be thankful for what we are expecting when we haven't yet received it. But we must trust that He has our best interest in His heart and that He never wants us to fail. Sometimes our asking is not that accurate, and we might be asking things that aren't in God's will. But He is a good God worthy of praise and thanksgiving, not because of what we want from Him but because of who He is.

Psalm 34:8 says,

> Oh, taste and see that *the Lord is good*! Blessed is the man who takes refuge in him!

Psalm 106:1 says,

> Praise *the Lord*! Oh give thanks to *the Lord*, for he *is good*, for his steadfast love endures forever!

The relearning process starts with the understanding that He is a good God and wants the best for us. We will learn more of this by searching the Scriptures daily to learn about His nature and attributes. This daily Bible study gets us into a place of learning to give thanks in faith before we receive.

I have had to learn to trust Him as I have been living by faith without any regular income for over thirteen years. I have learnt to thank Him in anticipation of Him coming through for me on a daily basis. I have learnt to be thankful before the blessing comes through, when it comes through and when it doesn't come through at all.

But I was in the advertising, marketing and print production business for about fifteen years before I answered the call to be an advocate for children in poverty and for children affected by the Aids virus through our charity The Fathers Blessing.

I worked in the production of annual reports for banks and multinationals. The Lord blessed me immensely in my company and gave me the ability to be an enabler and steward in the Kingdom to facilitate the work of the ministry. My substance was used greatly in the advancement the Kingdom.

It was a season of favour when the Lord moved in miraculous ways. I could share many testimonies of God's providence from my time in the marketplace even though I wasn't very much aware of our need to be positioned as gatekeepers in the marketplace. For example, a bank wanted

THANKSGIVING BRINGS MULTIPLICATION

to produce their annual report, and I was invited to bid for the job on behalf of our agency. The submitted designs were to be presented first to the Corporate Affairs Manager, then to the Managing Director/CEO and finally to the Board of Directors for a final approval before the contract would be awarded.

There were two main criteria: first design which involved the cover and the layout of the inside pages, and second, the production cost. At every stage, their Corporate Affairs Manager advised the CEO on the various designs from the agencies. The Corporate Affairs Manager told me that my designs were not likely to pass the first stage. However, he was obliged to make a presentation for it to the CEO. On the presentation there were managers in the room who were not normally part of the process. The CEO asked for their opinions and they all preferred our design. Only the Corporate Affairs Manager objected simply because he wanted to give the job to his preferred agency.

However, this was not the end of the process, as the designs still had to be presented to the board without any prejudice. So, I was invited to present our bid to the board, and the Corporate Affairs Manager bombarded me with hostile questions. But I stayed calm and maintained professional demeanour.

My understanding was that the advice and the input of this manager was integral to the decision, however the board would make the final decision.

To my utter amazement and after many days of prayers, we were offered the job. The job was very profitable and enabled us to get high exposure in this market. But what I want to highlight is that God's favour was on me. This manager had always gotten away with influencing not only the CEO but the Board of Directors who would get the jobs and was not pleased about us getting it. Whatever financial arrangement he had with his choice agency was obviously very beneficial for him!

On the day that I went to sign the contract, I got to the reception and asked for the Corporate Affairs Manager. I was invited into the office only to find out there was a different person on the seat to give me the purchase order. When I inquired about the Corporate Affairs Manager, I heard that he had been fired and that signing my purchase order had been his last assignment! When God is on your side, there is no power in hell that can stop you!

My season now for more than twenty years has been training and learning more about the ways of God, especially in the areas of finance and what it is meant to accomplish for the Kingdom. I have learnt and known what it is to abound and to be abased, as Paul rightly puts it in Philippians 4:12-13,

THANKSGIVING BRINGS MULTIPLICATION

I know what it means to lack, and I know what it means to experience overwhelming abundance. For I'm trained in the secret of overcoming all things, whether in fullness or in hunger. And I find that the strength of Christ's explosive power infuses me to conquer every difficulty.

He has now been calling me back into the marketplace, and this is one of the reasons why I can write this book and hopefully be able to teach others and pass on to them how to walk in this role of marketplace gatekeeper. Deuteronomy 8:7-10 says,

> For the Lord your God is bringing you into a good land, a land of brooks of water, of fountains and springs, flowing out in the valleys and hills, a land of wheat and barley, of vines and fig trees and pomegranates, a land of olive trees and honey, a land in which you will eat bread without scarcity, in which you will lack nothing, a land whose stones are iron, and out of whose hills you can dig copper. And you shall eat and be full, and you shall bless the Lord your God for the good land he has given you.

The Lord has never failed on His promises. This is the assurance of faith that we have in Him that enables us to always give thanks. Joshua 21:45 says,

> Not one word of all the good promises that the Lord had made to the house of Israel had failed; all came to pass.

1 Kings 8:56 says,

> Blessed be the Lord who has given rest to his people Israel, according to all that he promised. Not one word has failed of all his good promise, which he spoke by Moses his servant.

If He has not failed the children of Israel, He will never fail you either! This is more than enough for us to give thanks even when we are still waiting for the manifestation of all that we are believing Him for.

Thanksgiving is foundational to everything you will do as a marketplace gatekeeper. You don't wait for something to happen to give thanks. You don't have to wait to get a promotion or get a raise to give thanks. You don't have to wait for that big contract to come through before you give thanks. It has been said that you must learn to keep praising the Lord in the corridor before you get to the door.

Ezra 3:11 (NIV) says about the laying of the Second Temple's foundation,

> With praise and thanksgiving they sang to the Lord: "He is good; his love toward Israel endures forever." And all the people gave a great shout of praise to the Lord, because the foundation of the house of the Lord was laid.

THANKSGIVING BRINGS MULTIPLICATION

The people gave thanks for the foundation of the house of the Lord—even before the house itself had been built. This means you set the foundation of everything you do with praise and thanksgiving.

What a way to begin a project!

Heaven is constantly giving thanks to the Lord. Revelation 7:11-12 says,

> And all the angels were standing around the throne and around the elders and the four living creatures, and they fell on their faces before the throne and worshiped God, saying, "Amen! Blessing and glory and wisdom and thanksgiving and honor and power and might be to our God forever and ever! Amen."

Give thanks at all times especially when you are waiting! Why? Because He is a good Father and wants the very best for us, and by thanking Him before you have received demonstrates that you know Him and trust in His faithfulness.

God is raising you up as a Kingdom treasurer that He can trust with the wealth and resources He puts in your hands. He is looking for gatekeepers in the marketplace, able to be good stewards.

CHAPTER 7
MOVING FROM SELF TO KINGDOM MENTALITY

> He also told them a parable: "No one tears a piece from a new garment and puts it on an old garment. If he does, he will tear the new, and the piece from the new will not match the old." (Luke 5:36)

When we begin to understand why we are called to be marketplace gatekeepers, a shift from self-centredness to Kingdom-mindedness must come in our mentality. And we must know our calling and begin to understand the area of society where the Lord would have us to have an influence.

The first call of every believer to be a follower of Jesus is already outlined in the Scriptures, and no matter what else God has called us to do, He has always called us to put His Word into practice. That is always the starting point.

MARKETPLACE GATEKEEPERS

1 Thessalonians 5:16-18 (ESV) says,

> Rejoice always, pray without ceasing, give thanks in all circumstances; for this is the will of God in Christ Jesus for you.

God is asking us to be full of joy, praying always with a grateful heart. This is God's will for us, which means that when you do that, you are on already on the road to grasping the will of God for your life.

But the will of God for our lives is more specific than that. One way to discover what the next step might be is to begin to discern the particular things in society that give you the most grief or resonate with your heart.

Your challenges can also often point to your calling. Overcoming them will often take you to a place where you will be able to help others overcome similar challenges. Also, your passion will often lead you directly to your purpose or calling.

With me, anytime I saw children in poverty I would start to cry uncontrollably and couldn't stop. Oftentimes this could happen even when I was watching TV with the ads from the different agencies or charities coming up and showing graphic images of malnourished children. Tears would start to roll down my eyes, and there was no doubt in my heart that I needed to do something beyond just giving money to these organisations.

And God is always ready to equip us once we know the area of our call. So, we started by sponsoring two children through a charity that enabled us to be part of the children's lives and give towards their care and education. We have been doing this for the last twelve years. We have watched and seen these two girls grow. They are now in secondary school, and I'm hoping we'll be able to visit them and see them at some point. However, this was not enough for us. We wanted to be able to have more impact, and we started to get more detailed ideas about what to do.

Eventually, the Lord prompted us to start a charity helping Aids orphans. As we were pondering on this and wondered how we were going to pay the lawyer to register the charity, someone gave us some money which was enough to register it. We called the charity The Father's Blessing, but we then we had the challenge of getting this approved through the Charity Commission. This was not something we could do on our own. But God in his faithfulness put us through a friend of ours who was willing to do this without any fees. Isn't God amazing? We have been running The Father's Blessing since 2007 and started with some of the proceeds of selling our apartment. There's always a sacrifice to be made!

We were struggling to make payments on our mortgage at the time, and our house was going to be repossessed, but the wisdom of the Lord was for us to sell and start the charity while we moved into a rented accommodation. It worked out well in the end.

This searching for your calling in prayer is often something that you must do on your own. After all, only you will be able to discover your destiny.

Some know it immediately, but others don't. But you will always know it at some point if you continue to seek the Lord. God will often find a scripture to guide you. The scripture we received for the charity was Isaiah 58:6-12.

When you begin to understand what your calling is, you must begin to transition into a new way of thinking. Your priorities must change for you to be able to move with the new.

There is a new perspective that you must have concerning how you can become a steward of what the Lord has given you. I call this a NEW day.

Jesus warns about not taking a bit of the old and attaching it to the new, as it would certainly destroy the new you are trying to cultivate.

The new is about understanding of what it is to be a marketplace gatekeeper. This comes with an awakening and urgency of God's plan for such things as the financing the Kingdom work of evangelising,

MOVING FROM SELF TO KINGDOM MENTALITY

caring for the orphans and widows and alleviating poverty.

There is a time for everything. But change can be difficult. No one wants the new, especially, if they have been used to a pattern or a way of life. Luke 5:39 says,

> And no one after drinking old wine desires new, for he says, "The old is good."

The old things are those things that are already working well and matured in our lives. But the old things shouldn't stop us from pursuing the new things of God. But Jesus says in Luke 5:37-38:

> And no one puts new wine into old wineskins. If he does, the new wine will burst the skins and it will be spilled, and the skins will be destroyed. But new wine must be put into fresh wineskins. The new fermenting wine will cause the old to stretch beyond its capacity and burst.

We need a new mind-set to move effectively in this new arena, as you cannot package the old in a new way. The old must go and give way for the new, and this is time sensitive! Jesus says in Luke 21:29-33 (ESV):

> Look at the fig tree, and all the trees. As soon as they come out in leaf, you see for yourselves and know that the summer is already near. So also, when you see

these things taking place, you know that the kingdom of God is near. Truly, I say to you, this generation will not pass away until all has taken place. Heaven and earth will pass away, but my words will not pass away.

There are so many things that are competing for our attention, but we must focus on our walk as Christians and as marketplace gatekeepers. The Kingdom of God is here, and we need to be ready to help those who are on the field bringing it to the world.

The Parable of the Ten Virgins shows us the importance of timing.

> Then the kingdom of heaven will be like ten virgins who took their lamps and went to meet the bridegroom. Five of them were foolish, and five were wise. For when the foolish took their lamps, they took no oil with them, but the wise took flasks of oil with their lamps.
>
> As the bridegroom was delayed, they all became drowsy and slept. But at midnight there was a cry, "Here is the bridegroom! Come out to meet him." Then all those virgins rose and trimmed their lamps. And the foolish said to the wise, "Give us some of your oil, for our lamps are going out." But the wise answered, saying, "Since there will not be enough for us and for you, go rather to the dealers and buy for yourselves."
>
> And while they were going to buy, the bridegroom came, and those who were ready went

> in with him to the marriage feast, and the door was shut. Afterward the other virgins came also, saying, "Lord, lord, open to us." But he answered, "Truly, I say to you, I do not know you." Watch therefore, for you know neither the day nor the hour. (Matthew 25:1-13 ESV)

No one knows the time, but certainly we must be prepared and ready to answer the call of being a marketplace gatekeeper!

We are told five of the virgins were foolish and five of them were wise. The difference between them is that the foolish virgins were not ready, and their lamps were not filled with oil. Are you ready? There is a season for everything, but often we postpone action, thinking that it can be done later. But we must be ready for no one knows the time. We are going to answer to the Lord on that day if we have done what He has required of us.

I am not so much as treating these verses as a word on the End Times but as an advice and an awareness on how timing affects what we are meant to do, fulfilling or negating our purpose of existence. Many Christians have passed on to the other side without ever accomplishing their dreams and purpose on earth. May it never happen to us!

Each one of those examples by Jesus has to do with timing and the response of those concerned. We can see how the timing of the response makes a difference to the outcome.

God is raising you up as a Kingdom treasurer that He can trust with the wealth and resources He puts in your hands. He is looking for gatekeepers in the marketplace, able to be good stewards.

Being successful in the marketplace does not exclude you from the fellowship in the church and does not place you above the brother or sister who is not in a high position. Instead, it is a position of humility and honour when God uses us in this way. But principally, we must be vigilant against materialism, because quite often we allow the cares of this life to overtake and weigh us down so much that we forget our purpose on earth.

WATCH YOURSELVES
Jesus says in Luke 21:34-36,

> But watch yourselves lest your hearts be weighed down with dissipation and drunkenness and cares of this life, and that day come upon you suddenly like a trap. For it will come upon all who dwell on the face of the whole earth. But stay awake at all times, praying that you may have strength to escape all these things that are going to take place, and to stand before the Son of Man.

Jesus says in Luke 12:15-21,

MOVING FROM SELF TO KINGDOM MENTALITY

"Take care, and be on your guard against all covetousness, for one's life does not consist in the abundance of his possessions." And he told them a parable, saying, "The land of a rich man produced plentifully, and he thought to himself, 'What shall I do, for I have nowhere to store my crops?' And he said, 'I will do this: I will tear down my barns and build larger ones, and there I will store all my grain and my goods. And I will say to my soul, "Soul, you have ample goods laid up for many years; relax, eat, drink, be merry."' But God said to him, 'Fool! This night your soul is required of you, and the things you have prepared, whose will they be?' So is the one who lays up treasure for himself and is not rich toward God."

God wants our hearts, and they are more important to Him than anything else. So, if you are reading this book, and you are in the marketplace, but you have not yet surrendered your life to the Lord, there is not a better time than now. Call upon God and surrender your heart to Him, acknowledge your sins to Him, ask Him to forgive you and accept Jesus into your heart.

We are to lay up our treasures for the Lord to accomplish Kingdom purposes, and in the end the Lord will be able to say to us, "Well done, good servant! Because you have been faithful in a very little, you shall have authority over ten cities." (Luke 19:17)

We need a completely new mind-set and renewal in our ways of thinking. We must forsake our old ways, which do not have an eternal perspective and don't achieve the Kingdom purposes. We are not of ourselves but belong to God, and while He has given all things for our enjoyment, we must never lose sight of the real purpose of why we are here on earth and the reasons behind our blessing.

―⚜―

Worship is primarily not about singing in church, it is what we do when no one is watching. Worshipping extravagantly is something we must imbibe. We worship God in Spirit but also with our substance!

―⚜―

CHAPTER 8
WORSHIP IN SPIRIT AND IN TRUTH

> And he said to him, "You shall love the Lord your God with all your heart and with all your soul and with all your mind. This is the great and first commandment. And a second is like it: You shall love your neighbor as yourself. On these two commandments depend all the Law and the Prophets." (Matthew 22:37-40)

Loving God with all your heart and your neighbour as yourself is the beginning of worship. Jesus didn't invent these commandments but referred to Deuteronomy 6:5 and Leviticus 19:18. These two commandments were already in the Mosaic Law and demonstrate the continuity between the Old and the New Testament.

Our primary duty as a marketplace gatekeeper is to love God. This is not about going to church every Sunday, or assuming that if you are the choirmaster it must automatically mean that you love the Lord.

Instead, it is about being intentional in your act of worship to the Lord. It is about having faith in Him and being devoted to Him. Loving God is the great and the first commandment. So above everything else—even for a gatekeeper in the marketplace—is to love God with total and absolute devotion. Then Jesus talks about loving our neighbour just as we love ourselves.

We are called to love God more than we love ourselves and neighbour as we love ourselves.

According to Jesus, every aspect of our lives is totally dependent on these two commandments. It is a short passage, and you can miss it if your Bible study is based on quantity reading. But we must pay extra attention to these verses, as they reveal the rationale behind the rest of the verses in much of the Bible.

I don't think most Christians have even begun to catch the enormity of these two commandments. I'm certain that most of us love ourselves a bit more than anyone else, and perhaps our family members nearly as much as we love ourselves, but the circle of our love remains rather small. The evidence for this is in the proportion of the money we choose to spend for our non-urgent wants—things that aren't necessary—in comparison to what we give to others.

So, who is your neighbour? In Luke's version, the person who asked about the greatest commandment sought to justify himself and inquired for the definition of the word "neighbour". That was a fatal error, which nevertheless gave us one of the best-known parables —the story about the Good Samaritan.

> Jesus replied, "A man was going down from Jerusalem to Jericho, and he fell among robbers, who stripped him and beat him and departed, leaving him half dead. Now by chance a priest was going down that road, and when he saw him he passed by on the other side. So likewise a Levite, when he came to the place and saw him, passed by on the other side.
>
> But a Samaritan, as he journeyed, came to where he was, and when he saw him, he had compassion. He went to him and bound up his wounds, pouring on oil and wine. Then he set him on his own animal and brought him to an inn and took care of him. And the next day he took out two denarii and gave them to the innkeeper, saying, 'Take care of him, and whatever more you spend, I will repay you when I come back.' Which of these three, do you think, proved to be a neighbor to the man who fell among the robbers?" He said, "The one who showed him mercy." And Jesus said to him, "You go, and do likewise." (Luke 10:30-36)

This is a classic example of how we can miss the opportunity to love our neighbour. Some might think that the neighbour is the one that lives next to your house or on your street, which is not entirely wrong, as they are included, but Jesus expands the definition even to those that you don't even know or have never met before.

In this story the priest and the Levite that are knowledgeable about the Law and the commandments of God are the ones that do not stop to help this man that had been robbed and beaten. The priest and the Levite were so much caught up in themselves and in their legalistic requirements for ritual purity that they forgot that loving this man was a much greater requirement than anything else. They had read the Law and they would have been able to quote these same scriptures used by Jesus from memory without any problems at all. But were they putting into action the words they often quoted and read regularly?

It must not be so with us as marketplace gatekeepers. Our worship begins by loving God and our neighbour.

Again and again in the Bible we can see that true worship begins with sharing our substance. Mark 14:3-9 says,

> And while he was at Bethany in the house of Simon the leper, as he was reclining at table, a woman came with an alabaster flask of ointment of pure nard, very costly, and she broke the flask and poured it over his head. There were some who said to themselves indignantly, "Why was the ointment wasted like that? For this ointment could have been sold for more than three hundred denarii and given to the poor." And they scolded her.
>
> But Jesus said, "Leave her alone. Why do you trouble her? She has done a beautiful thing to me. For you always have the poor with you, and whenever

WORSHIP IN SPIRIT AND IN TRUTH

you want, you can do good for them. But you will not always have me. She has done what she could; she has anointed my body beforehand for burial. And truly, I say to you, wherever the gospel is proclaimed in the whole world, what she has done will be told in memory of her."

The woman broke her alabaster flask of good quality, pure nard and poured this very expensive ointment on Jesus. In today's value 300 denarii would be around $30,000. How would you feel if someone did that today?

You can only do this if you have the heart of total devotion to the person. She gave everything she had and didn't give any thought about holding back at all. This is an act of how our worship should be to the Lord: full-blown unpretentious, not holding back, an act of total and pure adoration.

Worship is primarily not about singing in a church, it is what we do when no one is watching. Worshipping extravagantly is something we must imbibe. We worship God in Spirit but also with our substance!

Jesus says in John 4:23-24,

> But the hour is coming, and is now here, when the true worshipers will worship the Father in spirit and truth, for the Father is seeking such people to worship him. God is spirit, and those who worship him must worship in spirit and truth.

There must be a sincerity of heart in how we worship the Lord hence the Bible says it must be in Spirit and in truth. Worship is not something you approach half-heartedly, it has to be whole or nothing.

When we operate in the marketplace, we must keep our eyes on the ball and not get distracted, as any distraction could be costly. Our focus must be on the Lord, who is our source and in whom we breathe and live and have our being. Worshipping the Creator of the Universe with full adoration is our reasonable service.

CIRCUMCISE YOUR HEART

> And now, Israel, what does the Lord your God require of you, but to fear the Lord your God, to walk in all his ways, to love him, to serve the Lord your God with all your heart and with all your soul, and to keep the commandments and statutes of the Lord which I am commanding you today for your good? Behold, to the Lord your God belong heaven and the heaven of heavens, the earth with all that is in it. (Deuteronomy 10:12-14)

The Temple gatekeepers were Levites. Levites were a tribe of singers and worshippers chosen by God. David placed them in charge of the Temple in anticipation of it being built by his son, King

WORSHIP IN SPIRIT AND IN TRUTH

Solomon, and they were in charge of the Treasuries and trusted to keep things in the House of God. 1 Chronicles 9:26 says,

> For the four chief gatekeepers, who were Levites, were entrusted to be over the chambers and the treasures of the house of God.

1 Chronicles 9:33 adds,

> Now these, the singers, the heads of fathers' houses of the Levites, were in the chambers of the temple free from other service, for they were on duty day and night.

You have to learn to worship day and night. David was a worshipper and knew from experience that every success was attributed to what he did in private with his harp, rendering worship to God, so he raised up worshippers and gatekeepers to serve in the house of the Lord. 1 Chronicles 23:5 says that

> 4,000 gatekeepers, and 4,000 shall offer praises to the Lord with the instruments that I have made for praise.

The Lord wants you to take charge and be the thermostat in the marketplace, so that everyone else will look at you and understand that you must be doing something right. We want to follow the same path of excellence and become the trailblazers in our chosen field.

Worship becomes your greatest weapon to stand firm against the sharks in the marketplace. The sharks want to destroy you, to malign you, and to get you out of the way. They don't like those with integrity and those who don't play their game, but you must come on the offensive with praise and worship to the Lord. Goliath will always point the sword at you just like he did with David. But you are about to use the sword of the giant to cut off his head! Worship is the ultimate weapon.

Jehoshaphat understood the power of worship very well. In 2 Chronicles 20:17-19 the prophet Jahaziel encourages King Jehoshaphat.

> "You will not need to fight in this battle. Stand firm, hold your position, and see the salvation of the Lord on your behalf, O Judah and Jerusalem. Do not be afraid and do not be dismayed. Tomorrow go out against them, and the Lord will be with you." Then Jehoshaphat bowed his head with his face to the ground, and all Judah and the inhabitants of Jerusalem fell down before the Lord, worshiping the Lord. And the Levites, of the Kohathites and the Korahites, stood up to praise the Lord, the God of Israel, with a very loud voice.

As soon as he heard the word of the Lord, he responded in worship and appointed singers as they went to face their enemy. 2 Chronicles 20:21-22 (ESV) says,

> And when he had taken counsel with the people, he appointed those who were to sing to the Lord and praise him in holy attire, as they went before the army, and say, "Give thanks to the Lord, for his steadfast love endures forever." And when they began to sing and praise, the Lord set an ambush against the men of Ammon, Moab, and Mount Seir, who had come against Judah, so that they were routed.

When you don't know what to do and you have no more words left, worship quietly, worship loudly, do it at home, do it in the open spaces, do it in the office and every available space and see what the Lord will do! You can't defeat your Goliath without coming from a place of loving the Lord in adoration and of worship and praise of His Holy name.

David had an absolute confidence in the Lord because of his love for Him. God loved him too and backed him in his endeavour; David was in no doubt at all that he would defeat Goliath.

1 Samuel 17:36-37 says:

> "Your servant has struck down both lions and bears, and this uncircumcised Philistine shall be like one of them, for he has defied the armies of the living God." And David said, "The Lord who delivered me from the paw of the lion and from the paw of the bear will

deliver me from the hand of this Philistine." And Saul said to David, "Go, and the Lord be with you!"

And God referred to David as a man after His own heart. Even in Acts 13:22 the apostle Paul testifies:

> And when he had removed him, he raised up David to be their king, of whom he testified and said, "I have found in David the son of Jesse a man after my heart, who will do all my will."

Can the Lord say that about you that you are a man after His heart?

The Lord appointed David as king over Israel. But long before this appointment was actualised, it was the testimony of David's life that opened the door to the king's court.

1 Samuel 16:15-17 says,

> And Saul's servants said to him, "Behold now, a harmful spirit from God is tormenting you. Let our lord now command your servants who are before you to seek out a man who is skillful in playing the lyre, and when the harmful spirit from God is upon you, he will play it, and you will be well." So Saul said to his servants, "Provide for me a man who can play well and bring him to me."

1 Samuel 16:18 says,

WORSHIP IN SPIRIT AND IN TRUTH

> One of the young men answered, "Behold, I have seen a son of Jesse the Bethlehemite, who is skillful in playing, a man of valor, a man of war, prudent in speech, and a man of good presence, and the Lord is with him."

David was skilful in playing the harp. It seemed to have been his main instrument for worship. This was the instrument that David used for worship while watching his father's sheep, and it was the same skill that brought David before King Saul. The king was often troubled with a harmful spirit, and it was the skill of David on his instrument that brought a temporary relief and healing to Saul.

We often get caught up in all that we want to do and forget about the source of everything that we need. We have to learn to choose the main thing or the ONE thing which is being at His feet and worshipping Him. Being at His feet simply means being intentional in spending time with Him in intimacy by worshipping, reading His Word, communing with Him and gaining more insight into what He has for you concerning your life principally and your business.

We can gain new strategies for our businesses from the position of worship.

Luke 10:38-42 says,

> Now as they went on their way, Jesus entered a village. And a woman named Martha welcomed him into her

house. And she had a sister called Mary, who sat at the Lord's feet and listened to his teaching. But Martha was distracted with much serving. And she went up to him and said, "Lord, do you not care that my sister has left me to serve alone? Tell her then to help me." But the Lord answered her, "Martha, Martha, you are anxious and troubled about many things, but one thing is necessary. Mary has chosen the good portion, which will not be taken away from her."

Do not be anxious and troubled about too many things as Jesus highlighted to Martha even though what Martha was doing was not wrong, only the timing of it. What better time than to spend time with Jesus when He is in your home? We are carriers of His presence and we must recognise this and take time to spend time with Him. We can worship ourselves into our breakthroughs and into the open doors He has for us.

Choose the ONE thing today!

—⁂—

What do you have in your hands? What you have in your hands is more than enough to make a difference to your world and become a true steward that the Lord is inviting to become a marketplace gatekeeper.

—⁂—

CHAPTER 9
PARABLE OF THE TEN MINAS

> He said therefore, "A nobleman went into a far country to receive for himself a kingdom and then return. Calling ten of his servants, he gave them ten minas, and said to them, 'Engage in business until I come.' But his citizens hated him and sent a delegation after him, saying, 'We do not want this man to reign over us.'" (Luke 19:12-14)

Through the Parable of the Ten Minas Jesus is asking people to engage in his business until He returns. Isn't that what the life of a marketplace gatekeeper is?

In the parable this businessman is hated by everyone, and they don't want him to rule over them, yet they were prepared to take his money. He ignores this and chooses to give everyone a chance. He must have been aware of what the citizens thought about him, but, nevertheless, he expected his servants to be able to handle the work.

Luke 19:15-27 continues the story,

When he returned, having received the kingdom, he ordered these servants to whom he had given the money to be called to him, that he might know what they had gained by doing business. The first came before him, saying, "Lord, your mina has made ten minas more." And he said to him, "Well done, good servant! Because you have been faithful in a very little, you shall have authority over ten cities." And the second came, saying, "Lord, your mina has made five minas." And he said to him, "And you are to be over five cities." Then another came, saying, "Lord, here is your mina, which I kept laid away in a handkerchief; for I was afraid of you, because you are a severe man. You take what you did not deposit, and reap what you did not sow." He said to him, "I will condemn you with your own words, you wicked servant! You knew that I was a severe man, taking what I did not deposit and reaping what I did not sow? Why then did you not put my money in the bank, and at my coming I might have collected it with interest?" And he said to those who stood by, "Take the mina from him, and give it to the one who has the ten minas." And they said to him, "Lord, he has ten minas!" "I tell you that to everyone who has, more will be given, but from the one who has not, even what he has will be taken away. But as for these enemies of mine, who did not want me to reign over them, bring them here and slaughter them before me."

The Lord will always give to us according to our ability, and there is always an expectation for us to deliver based on our abilities and even beyond them—when we put our trust in Him. We must learn to

PARABLE OF THE TEN MINAS

trust more in what the Lord can do through us and not so much in our own ability. When God gives you the ability, you can do much more despite your lack of qualifications or any other hindrances.

Exodus 31:2-6 shows how God anoints our skills.

> See, I have called by name Bezalel the son of Uri, son of Hur, of the tribe of Judah, and I have filled him with the Spirit of God, with ability and intelligence, with knowledge and all craftsmanship, to devise artistic designs, to work in gold, silver, and bronze, in cutting stones for setting, and in carving wood, to work in every craft. And behold, I have appointed with him Oholiab, the son of Ahisamach, of the tribe of Dan. And I have given to all able men ability, that they may make all that I have commanded you.

God put His Spirit in Bezalel and Oholiab, so they were able to build the Ark of the Covenant. There is no greater work that any man can engage in than to build what represents the presence of the Lord! They were chosen not because they had put in a job application on time but because of their skills. They were headhunted by the Lord! They were headhunted because they met all the requirements to construct the Ark of the Covenant of the Lord.

Exodus 36:1 says,

> Bezalel and Oholiab and every craftsman in whom the Lord has put skill and intelligence to know how

to do any work in the construction of the sanctuary shall work in accordance with all that the Lord has commanded.

The most important attribute the Lord put in them was His Spirit, so they had the ability to interpret the plans as detailed to Moses. They didn't need anyone to come on a day-to-day basis to interpret the proposed design to them because they were now possessed by the Spirit of the Lord.

We all have the same Spirit that enables us to carry out what the Lord wants from us. But unless we submit to the Spirit of the Lord, we won't be able to carry out our various assignments.

While we are skilled and rightfully so in our various professions, we must learn to submit to the will of God for our lives.

There was no doubt that the nobleman expected some returns from his investment. I don't know why he gave some ten, some five and some only one mina, but it probably depended on their abilities. The interesting thing about this is that each person was able to double on their investments, and they earned a reward on top of the profit.

Luke 19:16-19 says,

> The first came before him, saying, "Lord, your mina has made ten minas more." And he said to him, "Well done, good servant! Because you have been faithful in

PARABLE OF THE TEN MINAS

a very little, you shall have authority over ten cities." And the second came, saying, "Lord, your mina has made five minas.'" And he said to him, "And you are to be over five cities."

When we are faithful in the little that the Lord has positioned in our hands, there will be an increase in the authority to prosper even more than we can ever imagine.

But Luke 19:20-21 says about the unfaithful servant:

> Then another came, saying, "Lord, here is your mina, which I kept laid away in a handkerchief; for I was afraid of you, because you are a severe man. You take what you did not deposit, and reap what you did not sow.'"

But is what the unfaithful servant said true? No, as he was given the same chance that the others had but failed to deliver on the opportunity.

Luke 19:22-23 records the nobleman's response.

> He said to him, "I will condemn you with your own words, you wicked servant! You knew that I was a severe man, taking what I did not deposit and reaping what I did not sow. Why then did you not put my money in the bank, and at my coming I might have collected it with interest?"

At least the servant should have deposited the money in the bank, so an interest could have been earned without the servant having to work for it at all. But the wicked servant didn't bother to do even that.

The nobleman collected what was in the wicked servant's hands and gave it to the faithful servant who had the highest returns.

> And he said to those who stood by, "Take the mina from him, and give it to the one who has the ten minas." And they said to him, "Lord, he has ten minas!" "I tell you that to everyone who has, more will be given, but from the one who has not, even what he has will be taken away." (Luke 19:24-26)

Some complained about this action, but the nobleman knew that the one that had the capability to do a lot more than envisaged would also be capable of turning around the added one he was also given.

The lesson is that we do not have to have much to be able to bring in the harvest, but as we remain faithful in our business, the Lord begins to add more to us and there's increase in the yield.

It should be clear that this parable refers to Jesus Himself as the nobleman. Hence, we should take it very seriously.

What do you have in your hands? What you have in your hands is more than enough to make a difference to your world and for you to become a true steward

PARABLE OF THE TEN MINAS

that the Lord is inviting to become a marketplace gatekeeper.

PRAYER
Lord, I come humbly before You. Use all that I have to bring glory to Your Name. I ask that you anoint me with Your Spirit to be able to do all that You require of me to the glory of Your Name. Amen.

Let there be increase in my life for the expansion of Your Kingdom on earth in Jesus' mighty name. Amen.

No servant can serve two masters, for either he will hate the one and love the other, or he will be devoted to the one and despise the other. You cannot serve God and money. (Luke 16:13)

CHAPTER 10
INTEGRITY AND KINGDOM WEALTH

> One who is faithful in a very little is also faithful in much, and one who is dishonest in a very little is also dishonest in much. If then you have not been faithful in the unrighteous wealth, who will entrust to you the true riches? And if you have not been faithful in that which is another's, who will give you that which is your own? No servant can serve two masters, for either he will hate the one and love the other, or he will be devoted to the one and despise the other. You cannot serve God and money. (Luke 16:10-13)

In one sense, this whole book is focused on faithfulness, as nearly everything about the call to be a marketplace gatekeeper is about being faithful in every aspect of your life.

Accepting the call to be a marketplace gatekeeper is a call to let your relationship to wealth to be transformed.

There's wealth and there are *true riches*. Wealth speaks about all that you have acquired. It is the Lord who gives us the ability to produce wealth.

Deuteronomy 8:18 (NIV) says,

> But remember the Lord your God, for it is he who gives you the ability to produce wealth, and so confirms his covenant, which he swore to your ancestors, as it is today.

I'm not discounting that some of us have gone to school to learn many necessary skills. Even the craftsmen that built the Tabernacle needed to be skilful. But the Lord still had to put His Spirit in them for them to be successful in their assignment. We must submit all that we want to do into the hands of God, so He can give us the ability to produce wealth whilst living in righteousness. And I can assure you that when God puts His hand in anything, the impact will be supernatural and the yield often greater.

Personally, I want everything I have to come from the Lord. I want to remember Him in everything, so that He will keep His covenant with me. I want Him to confirm His covenant with me by giving me the ability to produce wealth.

But true riches are about spiritual stewardship and our responsibility in walking in alignment with

INTEGRITY AND KINGDOM WEALTH

God's Kingdom, which ultimately brings a heavenly reward. When it comes to finances, whatever we keep on earth, stays on earth. It is only what we give away that can bring us an everlasting reward.

Jesus says in Luke 16:13,

> No servant can serve two masters, for either he will hate the one and love the other, or he will be devoted to the one and despise the other. You cannot serve God and money.

This verse makes it abundantly clear that we cannot serve God and mammon at the same time. In the end, you will be forced to devote yourself to one or the other. Jeremiah 25:6 says,

> Do not go after other gods to serve and worship them, or provoke me to anger with the work of your hands. Then I will do you no harm.

Do not let the work of your hands become your object of worship. Do not provoke the Lord! Deuteronomy 5:7 says,

> You shall have no other gods before me.

Our wealth is to serve humanity and the Kingdom of God, and the Lord will not cease to bless us with more when we are found faithful. You must have the utmost devotion to the one who gave you the ability to make wealth. And the partnership with Him is far more glorious than financial wealth.

When you serve God rather than money, you will be walking in integrity with what the Lord has given to you, and the Lord will certainly promote you to the next level in His Kingdom and elevate you to a place of prominence. Proverbs 22:29 says,

> Do you see a man skillful in his work? He will stand before kings; he will not stand before obscure men.

We mustn't put a limit as to how far the Lord can bless us by serving our greed rather than Him.

So then, there remains a Sabbath rest for the people of God, for whoever has entered God's rest has also rested from his works as God did from his.
(Hebrews 4:9–10)

CHAPTER 11
REST

The command to rest is nothing new. It goes as far back as the work of creation itself. It was instituted by God for us all and started with God Himself.

Genesis 2:1–3 says,

> Thus the heavens and the earth were finished, and all the host of them. And on the seventh day God finished his work that he had done, and he rested on the seventh day from all his work that he had done. So God blessed the seventh day and made it holy, because on it God rested from all his work that he had done in creation.

There are two aspects to rest. First, there is the physical Sabbath rest. Then there is the rest from works, or an assurance of the finished work.

The Sabbath rest is physical rest, and the rest from works a state of the hope and the assurance of what God has done for us. As marketplace gatekeepers we need to be intentional about both. There is a rest after working through the week and there is a rest through the finished work of Christ, which is a state of mind.

REST AFTER WORK (SABBATH)

The Lord began the work of creation, and it took place in six days with the creation of man on the sixth day. And the Lord rested on the seventh day after He had finished the work.

The Lord then blessed the seventh day and made it holy. The church has moved away from this command, as the seventh day which is the Sabbath has become more of a working and partying day for many of us. It is no longer a holy day when we rest, refresh and spend time with family, as God intended for us.

I have tried to put this into practice often without much success, but when I have succeeded, I have found it quite refreshing and positive. In the times of Jesus, the Sabbath was observed in Israel, and it is still observed there today. Everything stops, there is no buying or selling, all the shops are closed, and all public transport stops. This is observed from sundown Friday till sundown Saturday. The practising Jews go to the synagogue and worship and read the Torah.

Matthew 12:8 says,

> For the Son of Man is lord of the Sabbath.

REST

Sometimes Sabbath can be twisted into a religious requirement with many commandments and prohibitions, so that even doing good works is banned. But this is nothing new. Jesus chastened the Pharisees and the religious leaders who had made the Sabbath into something it was never meant to be.

Mark 3:1-6 says,

> Again he entered the synagogue, and a man was there with a withered hand. And they watched Jesus, to see whether he would heal him on the Sabbath, so that they might accuse him. And he said to the man with the withered hand, "Come here." And he said to them, "Is it lawful on the Sabbath to do good or to do harm, to save life or to kill?" But they were silent. And he looked around at them with anger, grieved at their hardness of heart, and said to the man, "Stretch out your hand." He stretched it out, and his hand was restored. The Pharisees went out and immediately held counsel with the Herodians against him, how to destroy him.

The Sabbath was made for man and not man for the Sabbath. In Luke 13 Jesus is found again healing someone in Sabbath. He says in Luke 13:16:

> And ought not this woman, a daughter of Abraham whom Satan bound for eighteen years, be loosed from this bond on the Sabbath day?

Jesus healed the woman on the Sabbath. Having a time of rest does not preclude us from doing good.

Jesus says in Luke 14:5-6,

> "Which of you, having a son or an ox that has fallen into a well on a Sabbath day, will not immediately pull him out?" And they could not reply to these things.

Jesus didn't object to the commandment to rest on the Sabbath day, but He performed a lot of miracles on the Sabbath to dispel the myth that not even good works should be done on that day.

John 9:14-17 says,

> Now it was a Sabbath day when Jesus made the mud and opened his eyes. So the Pharisees again asked him how he had received his sight. And he said to them, "He put mud on my eyes, and I washed, and I see." Some of the Pharisees said, "This man is not from God, for he does not keep the Sabbath." But others said, "How can a man who is a sinner do such signs?" And there was a division among them. So they said again to the blind man, "What do you say about him, since he has opened your eyes?" He said, "He is a prophet."

And thereafter Jesus exposed their hypocrisy by highlighting the fact that they did do some work on Sabbath.

He says in John 7:22-24,

REST

> Moses gave you circumcision (not that it is from Moses, but from the fathers), and you circumcise a man on the Sabbath. If on the Sabbath a man receives circumcision, so that the law of Moses may not be broken, are you angry with me because on the Sabbath I made a man's whole body well? Do not judge by appearances, but judge with right judgment."

Sabbath is meant for the good of humanity without the religiosity that it has been turned into. I believe that the Sabbath rest is beneficial without the religious rules and regulations attached to it. Very often in the world we do not take a break, and often in the financial sector those who do are seen as wimps, and not putting all the hours in can be harmful to your career progress.

Sabbath is a good time to read and study the Scriptures, worship and switch off the phone and all work-related equipment like laptops. You'll be surprised how rejuvenated you will feel after a day's rest! It is often difficult in our age where most parties and celebrations are fixed for Saturdays, but I would encourage you to do it as often as you can.

C. H. Spurgeon said,

> Rest time is not waste time. It is economy to gather fresh strength . . . It is wisdom to take occasional furlough. In the long run, we shall do more by sometimes doing less.

SPIRITUAL REST

The Good News includes the revelation and deliverance found in the Lord Jesus, the New Covenant He established through His high-priestly sacrifice and the hope of eternity with Him.

The rest we are encouraged to enter is the assurance that Jesus has completed the work and we do not need to do anything to earn our salvation.

Jesus came to accomplish and finish all that the Father had planned for eternity, and we are simply asked to enter the rest.

Hebrews 4:4 says,

> For he has somewhere spoken of the seventh day in this way: "And God rested on the seventh day from all his works."

And we can only enter this rest by faith. But Hebrews 4:6 says,

> Since therefore it remains for some to enter it, and those who formerly received the good news failed to enter because of disobedience.

It seems that some people don't want to enter this rest! It is a gift, but some people don't want to enter it, because it entails submitting to God's will. This rest is about trusting God because of all that has been accomplished through creation and the sending of

REST

Jesus to redeem us. This is something we must enter through a renewed mind.

Hebrews 4:9-10 says,

> So then, there remains a Sabbath rest for the people of God, for whoever has entered God's rest has also rested from his works as God did from his.

God has ceased from His works ever since, and so should we, because Jesus accomplished it all on the cross. This can be difficult for some of us to believe, especially if we are going through difficulties and challenges, and our trust and faith in the Lord can sometimes diminish with us constantly asking if the Lord is with us at all. When what we are seeing in the physical does not tally with what we have read in the Word of God, and all hell seems to be breaking loose, we often begin to doubt, and the enemy will use this as a weapon against us. When we are in this position, we are encouraged to strive to renew our minds and rest in the accomplished work of the cross. Hebrews 4:11 says,

> Let us therefore strive to enter that rest, so that no one may fall by the same sort of disobedience.

It is a paradox that we must sometimes strive to enter the rest, but this is an appeal again for us once again to exercise faith. Let us approach the Lord with boldness knowing that all we need has already been given through Jesus Christ!

As Hebrews 4:16 says,

> Let us then with confidence draw near to the throne of grace, that we may receive mercy and find grace to help in time of need.

The writer of Hebrews knows that our natural mind has difficulties in receiving this assurance, and hence he repeats the appeal. We must therefore persevere in seeking that rest even when things don't tie up. He remains faithful and will never fail us. The only thing that can stop us is lack of faith and disobedience.

John 19:30 says,

> When Jesus had received the sour wine, he said, "It is finished," and he bowed his head and gave up his spirit.

You might think that you must strive because you have just started. But in Christ you have already finished because He has already finished.

We need to recognise the seasons that we are in and be discerning to know that our time here on earth is temporal. We must get on with the business of the Kingdom while we still have the time.

CHAPTER 12
CAST YOUR NETS ON THE OTHER SIDE

> And Simon answered, "Master, we toiled all night and took nothing! But at your word I will let down the nets." (Luke 5:5)

Simon was a professional fisherman who obviously knew a thing or two about fishing. He knew the timings of when to catch a big haul. There is a skill that comes with the timing and having to have a close watch on the tide. Simon ran a serious commercial venture. But he had toiled all night to have a catch with no results. This was evidently not a good day for them. It says in Luke 5:2:

> And he saw two boats by the lake, but the fishermen had gone out of them and were washing their nets.

Simon and his colleagues had resigned for the day and were washing and preparing their nets so they could try another day. But Jesus came to where they were and requested that they push the boat out again, so that He could carry out His assignment, which was to preach the Gospel to all those that were around. Yet hidden was the fact that He was just about to call His disciples for even a greater assignment and that call would revolutionize their lives. Luke 5:3 says,

> Getting into one of the boats, which was Simon's, he asked him to put out a little from the land. And he sat down and taught the people from the boat.

Jesus began with the preaching of the Gospel, as there were many people who were following Him and wanted to hear the word of eternal life.

Just before this, it says in Luke 5:1:

> On one occasion, while the crowd was pressing in on him to hear the word of God, he was standing by the lake of Gennesaret.

After Jesus had finished teaching the people, He gave an instruction to Simon Peter who was later going to be one of His faithful disciples.

> And when he had finished speaking, he said to Simon, "Put out into the deep and let down your nets for a catch." (Luke 5:4)

CAST YOUR NETS ON THE OTHER SIDE

This was certainly not the kind of instruction that the fishermen were expecting. So, Simon pointed out the obvious. Perhaps he thought that Jesus knew nothing about fishing as He was a carpenter. Nevertheless, he must have respected Jesus, as he followed His advice.

> And Simon answered, "Master, we toiled all night and took nothing! But at your word I will let down the nets." (Luke 5:5)

One of the most important parts of this story was the willingness of Peter to listen to Jesus, despite his professional skills and knowledge of fishing. This could have been the result of Jesus teaching on faith. Just imagine what would have made Peter to say those life-changing words: "But at your word". Those words evoked the power of change that gave way to the miraculous encounter that was totally life-changing for Peter and the other fishermen. They obeyed Jesus and cast their nets exactly where He instructed them to, and something happened that could only have been supernatural.

Luke 5:6–9 says,

> And when they had done this, they enclosed a large number of fish, and their nets were breaking. They signaled to their partners in the other boat to come and help them. And they came and filled both the boats, so that they began to sink. But when Simon

Peter saw it, he fell down at Jesus' knees, saying, "Depart from me, for I am a sinful man, O Lord." For he and all who were with him were astonished at the catch of fish that they had taken.

Sometimes, we have toiled all night, caught nothing and our businesses have taken a hit. Our endeavours have turned pear-shaped and we have given up. If that is the case, then it is time for you to invite Jesus to come and speak His word over your business and situation! When it seems all is lost, He is there in much more real way than we can ever imagine. When you have done all that you are able to do within your human capacity and you are about to fold your nets, then it's time to call on Jesus, who is ever near to step into the situation. And He will speak to you about where to cast your nets. We are bound to have hiccups in our businesses and enterprises, and when they do come, one way to mitigate against disaster is to call upon Him. And He will answer you.

Matthew 24:32–35 says,

> From the fig tree learn its lesson: as soon as its branch becomes tender and puts out its leaves, you know that summer is near. So also, when you see all these things, you know that he is near, at the very gates. Truly, I say to you, this generation will not pass away until all these things take place. Heaven and earth will pass away, but my words will not pass away.

The lesson of the fig tree is about timing. It is imperative that we have an idea of God's timing for our lives and why we need to do what we need to do because time is not promised for everything.

We need to recognise the seasons that we are in and be discerning to know that our time here on earth is temporal. We must get on with the business of the Kingdom while we still have the time.

What are you doing to bring about the manifestation of the Kingdom in your sphere of life and society? And while you are at it, remember the one who gave you the wealth and the one that must be revered and worshipped. While it is good to leave an inheritance for our children, we must not withhold it when it is in our power to release, share and be generous.

1 Timothy 6:17-19 says,

> As for the rich in this present age, charge them not to be haughty, nor to set their hopes on the uncertainty of riches, but on God, who richly provides us with everything to enjoy. They are to do good, to be rich in good works, to be generous and ready to share, thus storing up treasure for themselves as a good foundation for the future, so that they may take hold of that which is truly life.

This takes us to the parable of the rich fool, as the Bible aptly puts it. We must be mindful of the times and get on with the business of advancing the Kingdom of

God. Luke 12:13-21 says,

> Someone in the crowd said to him, "Teacher, tell my brother to divide the inheritance with me." But he said to him, "Man, who made me a judge or arbitrator over you?" And he said to them, "Take care, and be on your guard against all covetousness, for one's life does not consist in the abundance of his possessions."
>
> And he told them a parable, saying, "The land of a rich man produced plentifully, and he thought to himself, 'What shall I do, for I have nowhere to store my crops?' And he said, 'I will do this: I will tear down my barns and build larger ones, and there I will store all my grain and my goods. And I will say to my soul, "Soul, you have ample goods laid up for many years; relax, eat, drink, be merry."'
>
> But God said to him, 'Fool! This night your soul is required of you, and the things you have prepared, whose will they be?' So is the one who lays up treasure for himself and is not rich toward God."

When you make Jesus the Captain of your boat, you are bound to get the right results in a timely and orderly manner. Have you prayed or consulted the Lord about the direction for the new venture, the timing, the name, the location and so on? Very often even we as Christians who should know better go ahead and do it before we ask the Lord to come and endorse it rather than allow Him to be part of the process right from the beginning.

CAST YOUR NETS ON THE OTHER SIDE

Whatever decision you make, let it be the one that brings the justice of God to the ills of society. We have a duty of care to the poor and to the disadvantaged. We are the hands and feet of Jesus.

Let Deuteronomy 15:7-11 be your guiding principle:

> If among you, one of your brothers should become poor, in any of your towns within your land that the Lord your God is giving you, you shall not harden your heart or shut your hand against your poor brother, but you shall open your hand to him and lend him sufficient for his need, whatever it may be. Take care lest there be an unworthy thought in your heart and you say, "The seventh year, the year of release is near," and your eye look grudgingly on your poor brother, and you give him nothing, and he cry to the Lord against you, and you be guilty of sin. You shall give to him freely, and your heart shall not be grudging when you give to him, because for this the Lord your God will bless you in all your work and in all that you undertake. For there will never cease to be poor in the land. Therefore I command you, "You shall open wide your hand to your brother, to the needy and to the poor, in your land."

Our heavenly father is a generous God, and this must be reflected in our lives and conduct as gatekeepers in the marketplace.

BY DR. GEORGE ANNADORAI

ECONOMIC EVANGELISM
THROUGH THE CHURCH IN THE MARKETPLACE

ECONOMIC EVANGELISM

THE CHURCH IN THE MARKETPLACE AS ONE CIRCLE IN THE BOOK OF ACTS

THE CHURCH VS. THE MARKETPLACE AS TWO CIRCLES POLARIZED AGAINST ONE ANOTHER
(AD 500 – 1500)

THE CHURCH & THE MARKETPLACE KISSING ONE ANOTHER TODAY
(AD 1998 TO 2018)

THE CHURCH IN THE MARKETPLACE ONCE AGAIN TOMORROW
(AD 2019 & BEYOND)

MARKETPLACE GATEKEEPERS

As part of His end-time plan and His eternal purpose Jesus is presently building an economic superhighway that stretches all the way from the Far East aka Pacific/Asia (end of the earth) to the Middle East aka Jerusalem, Israel (centre of the earth) and beyond in fulfilment of an ancient prophecy hidden in the Book of Isaiah 62:10-12.

ECONOMIC EVANGELISM DEFINED

@Shalom Israel (Asia + Pacific) we define "economic evangelism" simply as using commerce to convert and trade to transform people and nations.

EARLY CHURCH AND ECONOMIC EVANGELISM

Acts 2
Acts 3
Acts 4
Acts 5
Acts 6

ECONOMIC EVANGELISM DESCRIBED

People and nations were converted to Christ and transformed by trade both in the Early Church (Book of Acts) and for the first 300 years after that. Tragically, as the Church dropped this God-given strategy Satan was quick to pick it up and began converting and transforming people and nations through commerce and trade. This was how Islam that was born in Saudi

ECONOMIC EVANGELISM

Arabia came to Asia creating the largest Islamic sectors in the world today in countries such as Indonesia and India.

Islam was not the only religion that was exported to the nations through trade. Buddhism also took the same road to spread their own version of the gospel. The time has finally come for the Church to reclaim its intellectual property called **economic evangelism**.

ECONOMIC EVANGELISM DEMONSTRATED

@ Shalom Israel (Asia Pacific) we want to capture, carry and communicate this truth to God's people everywhere in order that the *Church in the marketplace* may be re-born once again in our day and time in every city, community and country.

ECONOMIC EVANGELISM + DISCIPLESHIP

Today in the Church we separate evangelism and discipleship while we see these two as two sides of the same coin in the Early Church (Book of Acts), which was a church in the marketplace. **@Galilee experience** we will join these two together once again believing that what God has put together must remain together.

THE CHURCH IN THE MARKETPLACE

The end-time Church as it was in the Early Church

1. Jehovah & the Patriarchs
2. Jehovah & the nation of Israel
3. Jehovah & the Jewish people
4. Jesus as an entrepreneur
5. Jesus and His enterprise called the Church
6. Jesus and His enterprise called Israel
7. Jubilee Economic Model
8. Jesus and His band of entrepreneurs
9. Jews & Entrepreneurship
10. Jewish Laws (Torah)
11. Jewish Land (Torah)
12. Jewish Chutzpah
13. Jesus and the end-time Church

JESUS AND HIS CHURCH THEN & NOW

The apple has fallen far from the tree. The anointing and the authority are no longer with us.

The agenda of the Church in the Kingdom of God & the kingdom of Satan

ECONOMIC EVANGELISM

1940s: the rebirth of Israel
1960s: Demos Shakarian & the FGBMF
1980s: Bill Hamon and the saint's movement
2000s: the 7 mountain's movement
2020s: the Church in the marketplace once again!

Copyright 2019 by Dr. George Annadorai

www.ingramcontent.com/pod-product-compliance
Lightning Source LLC
LaVergne TN
LVHW041251080426
835510LV00009B/692